Poop, F

POOP, BOOZE, AND BIKINIS

First edition. February 5, 2014.

Written by Ed Robinson.

10 9 8 7 6 5 4 3 2 1

This book is dedicated to everyone who purchased Leap of Faith / Quit Your Job and Live on a Boat. Your support has encouraged me and is greatly appreciated.

Random Musings from a Liveaboard Boater

Ed Robinson

Table of Contents

Prelude

"Write what you know about" they say. Everyone is an expert on something. I don't know a whole lot about many things, but I do live on a boat, have for years. Certainly I've made some observations that may be helpful to others.

I've seen some things. I've screwed up a bunch. I've done some things right on occasion. Mostly I've observed. Some of the things I've learned are quite serious and useful, but no fun to write about. Instead I've chosen to focus on the fun, and the funny.

These are my random observations.

Poop

You landlubbers don't know how good you've got it. You hit the flusher and your poop magically disappears. It goes off through pipe land into some magical septic world never to be thought of again.

Not us boaters. We hold onto our poop. We keep it in a tank and carry it with us on our travels. We haul it all over paradise until we find someone willing to take it off our hands, so to speak.

We perfume it. We deodorize it. We experiment with various potions and powders in hopes of stopping the stink.

We know what a Y valve is. We know what a flapper valve is. Our toilet ain't a toilet. It's a head. We don't put toilet paper in it. We hang onto that too, carrying it around until it can be disposed of.

The head is maintained meticulously. It gets regular doses of vegetable oil to keep it lubricated. It is inspected almost daily, looking for leaks. It is cursed and it is worshipped. It is vital to our comfort and our survival so it is revered. It is apt to quit working at the worst times, so it is feared.

It reeks sometimes. It has a vent. Imagine sitting on your patio and when someone flushes in the house you get a good whiff of whatever they just sent down.

Imagine having a septic tank in your basement. Every time you go down there to do laundry or whatever, you get to see it. Once a week you drop deodorant/perfume in it. You smell it on the patio when someone flushes. Then occasionally you call someone to come pump it out.

Some unscrupulous boaters choose to flush directly overboard. Think about that the next time you decide to go swimming in the harbor with all the pretty sailboats.

Coastal cruisers can pump directly into the ocean if they are the legal distance off shore. It's legal. It's also quite unpleasant. Imagine hauling your house poop five miles offshore to get rid of it.

Boat heads are not private. There is no where you can go where you won't hear me, or smell me.

There is one Golden Rule in holding tank management: Never, ever, EVER let the holding tank overflow. Don't risk it. Do whatever is necessary to be certain it will not overflow. The resulting cleanup can only be called a shitty job. (Don't ask me how I know that.)

Bet you never thought about poop so much. That's my point exactly.

Close Encounters of the Turd Kind

Once upon a time there were four of us lounging in the water up to our chests. An object floated to us and my buddy picked it up, asking what was it? I said, "Dude, it's a turd". He very nonchalantly released it to continue floating on its merry way. We spent the next ten minutes discussing its possible origin. Eventually we decided that it must be a dog turd. That was probably wishful thinking but it worked for us at the time. (True Story)

Long ago there lived a seaman named Captain Bravo, a manly man who showed no fear when facing his enemies.

One day, while sailing the seas, the lookout yelled from the crow's nest that he had spotted a pirate ship. As the crew began to panic, Captain Bravo roared, "Bring me my red shirt!" The first mate quickly brought the red shirt to Captain Bravo. After donning the red shirt, Captain Bravo led his men into battle and they soundly defeated the pirates.

Later on that same day, the lookout spotted not one, but TWO pirate ships and yelled a battle alarm to the crew below! Captain Bravo again roared, "Bring me my red shirt!" Once again, though the battle was fierce, he and his crew were victorious!

That evening, as the men sat on deck recounting the day's triumphs, the first mate asked Captain Bravo, "Sir, why do you call for your red shirt before beginning to do battle?"

Captain Bravo replied, "If I am ever wounded in battle, the red shirt will prevent my blood from showing and thus, you men will continue to fight unafraid."

The men sat in silence, marveling at the courage of their Captain Bravo.

The next morning, just as dawn was breaking, the lookout spotted not one, not two, but EIGHT pirate ships approaching from the far horizon! Upon bellowing this information to the crew, every single man turned to look at Captain Bravo, waiting for his usual pre-battle command.

Without hesitation, Captain Bravo turned to his first mate and roared, "BRING ME MY BROWN PANTS!"

Why would I write a chapter for a book on poop? I even put poop in the title. It's like this. While writing this masterpiece of nautical humor, I've been operating the pump out boat for the city of Punta Gorda part-time. You see? Write what you know about. I think running a poop boat named SS Clearhead makes me an expert.

Marinas Versus Anchorages

What is good about a marina is what you miss when you are at anchor. Being plugged in to shore power is a big plus. Having unlimited water is nice too.

You can't run around naked in a marina, but you can take a shower whenever you want.

Marinas put neighbors on both sides of you, very close. They also protect you in bad weather.

Marinas have trash pickup, cable TV, free Wifi and swimming pools. Anchorages have manatees, dolphins, ospreys and really cool sunsets.

Marinas cost money. Anchoring is free.

Marinas house like-minded boat people. You can make lots of friends. Anchorages have real cruisers coming and going. You can make lots of *new* friends. The boating fraternity is full of nice people. You make friends quickly and easily. It also has its share of eccentrics. Don't judge.

Did I say anchoring is free?!

Marinas are in towns and cities. There is noise. Trash trucks at five a.m. Immigrant types mowing the grass at eight a.m. Fire trucks sirens, police sirens, general traffic noise and jets overhead. Anchorages sound like dolphins breath. Ospreys chirp from the island. Mullet jump and splash. Waves lap softly on your hull.

Living in a marina you see city sights, buildings, tourists and such. At anchor you see Pelicans diving on bait. At anchor you get a great sunset every night. You may have to leave the marina to catch a glimpse of the sunset.

Did I say marinas cost money?!

If you use the marinas facilities, you don't have to worry about your poop.

If you use the marinas facilities, you'll be sharing them with all the other marina occupants.

Marinas have rules. They expect a certain standard of living and behavior. At anchor you can do any damn fool thing you want.

If you live in a marina the scenery never changes. If you live at anchor, you can pull up anchor and change your scenery whenever you want.

I'm in a marina right now. Some strangers just walked up and down my finger pier ogling my boat. Nice enough folks but what about my privacy?

Don't get me started on day rooms. A day room is a shared facility in a marina, usually with a television. Think you can get six different sailors to agree on what to watch?

There's also a laundry room in marinas. That invariably means there is also a laundry Nazi. That's the woman who gets really pissed if someone leaves their laundry in the washer or dryer unattended. She is quick to throw your wet clothes out of "her" washer. She is equally quick to scold you when she finds out who the culprit is.

There is also a shared refrigerator. Don't leave an ice cream cake in the marina fridge. Someone will lick the icing off of it, (true story).

Dude just walked down my pier again. I had to run him off. For you marina novices, the main pier is okay. Do NOT walk down someone's finger pier. That would be like me walking up your driveway to look at your house.

Marinas cost money. Anchoring is free. Marina amenities are nice, but they cost money. Anchoring out gives you privacy, freedom, and the awesomeness of nature, and it's all for free.

Booze

We stick to the five o'clock rule. However, we amend that due to daylight savings time. When it gets dark early we start drinking at four.

Box-O-Wine is a perfect boat beverage. No glass bottles and easy to store.

No glass beer bottles allowed on our boat. We save up the cans and donate them to worthy causes. It's an incentive to drink more beer.

For the most part, boaters drink. Liveaboard boaters drink a lot.

Any tiny excuse for a celebration is cause for a drink. "I cleaned the waterline", I need a drink. The dinghy motor started on the first pull, "I'll drink to that." It didn't rain today. "Let's make a toast to no rain."

The preferred liquor for landlubbers seems to be tequila these days. The preferred liquor of liveaboard boaters is rum, by far. Must be a pirate thing.

It is not uncommon to fall out of your dinghy after too many rum drinks.

People think boaters go to bed early because there is nothing to do after dark. That is not the case at all. They go to bed early because they are drunk.

We have a designated rum locker on our vessel. We also have an ice maker, strictly for booze purposes. We think this makes us professionals. We are a step above your average amateur drinker.

We have taken the dinghy several miles to shore, hopped a bus several more miles to a store, just to buy booze. We once wandered around on foot for hours, looking for a liquor store.

Booze does not go bad. You can never overstock when it comes to booze.

Booze doesn't make you poop, but it does make you pee. We carry that in the same tank as the poop.

Sunsets are enhanced when you have a drink in your hand, proven fact.

Conversation improves after a few drinks, proven fact.

Booze is the duct tape of life.

Good Booze Story

We were on a bareboat charter in the British Virgin Islands. One day we found ourselves at the bar in The Bight, Norman Island (go figure). We were working on our second Painkiller when Kim sees all these buckets up over the bar. They were the kind a kid would use to play in the sand. They said "Pirates Cove, BVI" on them. She wanted one as a memento. I asked the bartender if we could purchase a bucket. He said nope. "Well what are they for?" I asked. He said you have to buy them filled with the drink of your choice. We thought that over for two seconds. "Okay, let us have a bucket of Painkillers."

A few minutes later we are at the water's edge, sitting in chaise lounges, holding a bucket of rum with two straws. The blue Caribbean Sea is lapping gently at our feet. In the water a woman lolls about in water up to her chin. When she emerges, we can't help but notice she is wearing nothing but tiny thong bottoms, no top. She takes the chaise next to us and basks in the sun. So there I was, on a picturesque beach with my lovely fiancé. I was holding a bucket of booze, seated with a topless pair of European boobies. I never wanted that moment to end.

Great Booze Story

(From the same trip, we drank a lot) We were moored off of Saba Rock in North Sound, Virgin Gorda. We grilled dinner on the boat but decided to go to the restaurant for drinks. Saba Rock is a one acre island with an upscale resort. As we arrived at the dock in our dinghy, a sharply uniformed attendant greeted us. "Will you be joining us for dinner?" she asked. "Nope," I replied, "just here for the booze." She laughed and directed us to the bar. As soon as we sat down, Kim showed off her brand new sparkling engagement ring. I had just proposed the day before. The bartender gets the attention of the entire place. "This couple just got engaged. First round is on me." In perfect synchronization we both said, "shots of Patron!"

As soon as we slammed our shot glasses down on the bar, the first customer says "second round is on me." Then a third chimed in. This continued until every single customer in the place bought us a round of Patron. The details are a bit fuzzy at this point, but I remember we laughed a lot and had a fantastic time with a bunch of strangers from around the globe. Finally we had to call it quits. Standing on the dock we looked out over the harbor for our boat. There were maybe fifty boats moored in the dark, almost all from the same charter company that we used. Guess what? Every boat looked identical to us. It was dark, we were fairly well stoned on fine tequila, and we had no idea which one was ours. All we could remember was the name of the boat. We set out in the dinghy, riding around North Sound reading names on transoms for what seemed like an hour. Eventually we hit the jackpot. We managed to board without falling in and still had enough energy to top off the evening in style. That was the night we invented the term Mad Monkey Sex.

Bikinis

The bikini is the greatest invention in the history of mankind, (or womankind).

Some women shouldn't wear bikinis.

Some women on boats like to sunbathe topless or even nude. This is what binoculars were made for.

Bikini watching tip: Wear mirrored or very dark sunglasses. It makes your ogling less obvious. Holding a book in front of you helps too.

Is your wife wearing a bikini? Remember that as you leer at some other dude's wife.

A thong is not a sandal or a flip flop.

My grandfather called bikini bottoms "nothing but a string betwixt her legs."

Certain peach or tan colored bikinis make a girl appear nude from a distance. This is another good time for binoculars.

Most anchorages feature many more gray haired retirees than young bikini babes.

Bikini watching tip: Don't stay on one beach, move around. Find the spots that serve up the best bikini viewing opportunities. Frequent those spots.

Weekends are always better than weekdays for bikini viewing.

She's somebody's daughter.

Ladies; men assume that if you are wearing a tiny bikini, you *want* to be ogled.

Bikini watching tip: Your wife knows what you're looking at.

Don't forget the sunscreen.

A 16-year-old girl bought herself a very tiny bikini. Very proud, she came home and put it on. She then showed her mother how she looked in it.

"What do you think mom?" she asked.

Her mother replied, "If I wore that when I was your age, you would be five years older."

Two priests were going to Hawaii on vacation and decided that they would make this a real vacation by not wearing anything that would identify them as clergy.

As soon as the plane landed, they headed for a store and bought some really outrageous shorts and shirts, sandals, sunglasses, etc.

The next morning, they went to the beach, dressed in their "tourist" garb and were sitting on beach chairs, enjoying a drink, the sunshine and the scenery.

Presently, a "drop dead gorgeous" blonde in a tiny bikini came walking straight toward them. They couldn't help but stare.

As she passed them she turned, smiled, and said: "Good morning father, good morning father." Nodding and addressing each of them individually.

They were both stunned; how in the world were they recognized as priests?

They went back to the store, bought even more outrageous outfits and again they settled on the beach in their chairs to enjoy the sunshine, etc.

After a while, the same gorgeous blonde, wearing a string bikini this time, came walking toward them again. (They were glad they had sunglasses, because their eyes were about to pop out of their heads).

Again, she approached them and greeted them individually: "good morning father", "good morning father" and started to walk away.

One of the priests couldn't stand it and said, "Just a minute young lady. Yes, we are priests, and proud of it, but I have to know, how in the world did YOU know?"

"Oh father, don't you recognize me? I'm Sister Kathryn!"

An old man went to a beach and sees a sexy girl in a bikini. He went up to her and asked her, "Can i feel your sexy, juicy boobs?"

The girl said, "No way, get away from me old man."

The guy said, "Twenty dollars?"

"No"

"One hundred dollars?"

"No"

"Two hundred dollars?"

"No"

"Five hundred dollars?"

The girl thought, what harm can it do? "Sure".

The girl loosened her bikini and the man slipped his hand in her bikini.

While feeling her sexy, juicy boobs, the guy said, "OH MY GOD, OH MY GOD, OH MY GOD"

The girl said, "why do you keep saying OH MY GOD?

While continuing feeling her sexy, juicy boobs, he said "OH MY GOD, where am i going to get five hundred dollars?"

Marine Critters

Manatees are very friendly. They will come right up to you and let you pet them. You are not supposed to touch manatees, but who can resist? Unfortunately, manatees are none too bright. The move very slowly or not at all, hovering just below the surface in the perfect target zone to get hit by a passing boat.

On the other hand, dolphins appear to be quite intelligent. I've had them hang around me while I was catching fish. A just released fish is easy prey for them. That's pretty smart if you ask me. I've had herons and pelicans do the same thing. We humans have a fondness for dolphins. We know they are smart and they seem so friendly. Not all of them are nice though. Just like people there are good dolphins and bad dolphins. Good dolphin sees you drowning and saves your life. Bad dolphin sees you drowning and decides now is a good time to hump you.

We've had several pet sea gulls. The first we named Jonathan after the book Jonathan Livingston Sea Gull. He eventually disappeared but we got a new one. I named him Steven, after Steven Seagal.

Any osprey is a better fisherman than me. Maybe I'd improve if not catching a fish meant not eating. Ospreys will chase competitors out of their territory. I've seen them harass pelicans, other ospreys and even eagles into leaving.

Random trivia: Dolphins sleep with half their brain. One half sleeps and the other half keeps them on autopilot so they can breathe and stay with their mates.

Snook like to hang out in the shade. They lurk under docks a lot. They won't move too far to chase down bait or a lure. Put it right in front of them and just dangle it there.

Redfish move on to flats during the first hour or two of an incoming tide.

Tarpon are the most frustrating fish ever. When they are not feeding, nothing will change their minds. When they are feeding they just break you off or throw the hook.

Fresh grouper is the perfect food. It's the best tasting fish that swims.

Gopher turtles live on islands but they can't swim. How'd they get there?

Sea turtles are terrible mothers. They just dump their eggs in the sand, bury them and swim away.

Political correctness tidbit: The goliath grouper used to be called the Jewfish. The black grouper is still called a black grouper.

Cormorants are called "goonie birds" on our boat. I've heard them called brown ducks. I've heard them called "water turkeys". Nobody calls them cormorants. They are a bird, but they can swim better than they can fly. An old friend called them submarine chiggens.

Pelicans are the Bassett Hounds of the aquatic seabird world. They are big, goofy looking, slow and just plain weird. It's a wonder they don't break their necks when diving on bait.

Snowy Egrets are professional beggars. They have no problem landing on any boat to beg for shrimp. They can tell a fishing boat from a pleasure boat too. I once had one land in the cockpit with me and try to steal my pop tart. We named him Herbie. Now we call all snowy egrets Herbie.

Otters are really cool.

Sharks are not cool at all, nor jellyfish, nor mosquitoes. Mosquitoes score the most bites. Jellyfish stings are more common than shark bites, but by golly I'll take a mosquito bite or jellyfish sting over a shark bite any day. There are lots of sharks in Florida. There used to be a huge hammerhead in the Boca Grande Pass named Hitler. The local guides hated Hitler, because he ate tarpon. The easiest tarpon for him to catch were those on an anglers line, or those exhausted after being released. I had this happen to me once. In spite of our efforts to shield our tarpon from the shark, Old Hitler won out and turned the water red with tarpon blood and scales.

My only other close encounter with a shark was while wade fishing on a sandbar off Cayo Costa. A guide boat had set up on the end of the bar. I was up to my waist in the Gulf and catching small ladyfish. Suddenly the guide says, "Big shark coming." I look over and see its dark shape crossing between me and the boat. To my credit I didn't panic. Instead I slowly and carefully started backing away to shallower water. The shark passed harmlessly by and continued down the coast. I was done with wade fishing that day however.

Sometimes shrimp jump out of the water and land in the dinghy. I find them in the morning. There is nothing worse than a shrimpy dingy.

Sometimes mullet jump out of the water and land in the dinghy. This does not usually end well for the mullet.

Really good eating fish never jump out of the water and land in the dinghy.

Sea Gulls love to poop on the dinghy.

Gators, there are plenty of them in Florida. Stay away from them. They are best viewed from a distance. All gator stories with bad endings start with the words "watch this."

I once had an interviewer ask me if I could be any animal, which would I choose? I said a dolphin. Here's what they do, feed on fish, play, and have sex. That sounds like a pretty good life to me.

Speaking of marine critters, no boating book would be complete without a parrot story or two.

A magician was working on a cruise ship in the Caribbean. The audience would be different each week, so the magician allowed himself to do the same tricks over and over again. There was only one problem: The captain's parrot saw the shows each week and began to understand how the magician did every trick. Once he understood he started shouting in the middle of the show:

"Look, it's not the same hat."

"Look, he is hiding the flowers under the table."

"Hey, why are all the cards the Ace of Spades?"

The magician was furious but couldn't do anything; it was, after all, the captain's parrot.

One day the ship had an accident and sank. The magician found himself adrift on a piece of wood in the middle of the ocean with the parrot, of course. They stared at each other with hate, but did not utter a word. This went on for a day, then another, and another.

After a week the parrot said: "OK, I give up. What'd you do with the ship?"

There's this sailor with a pet parrot. But the parrot swears like an old sea captain. He can swear for five minutes straight without repeating himself! Trouble is, the sailor who owns him is a quiet, conservative type, and this bird's foul mouth is driving him crazy. One day, it gets to be too much, so the sailor grabs the bird by the throat, shakes him really hard, and yells, "QUIT IT!" But this just makes the bird mad and he swears more than ever.

Then the sailor locks the bird in a kitchen cabinet. This really aggravates the bird and he claws and scratches everything inside. Finally the sailor lets the bird out. The bird cuts loose with a stream of vulgarities that would make a veteran seaman blush. The sailor is so mad that he throws the bird into the freezer. For the first few seconds there is a terrible racket from inside. Then it suddenly gets very quiet. At first the sailor just waits, but then he starts to think that the bird may be hurt. He's opens up the freezer door. The bird calmly climbs onto the man's outstretched arm and says, "Awfully sorry about the trouble I gave you. I'll do my best to improve my vocabulary from now on." The man is astounded. He can't understand the transformation that has come over the parrot.

The parrot speaks again, "By the way, what did the chicken do?"

Boats

There are more kinds of boats then there are kinds of cars. In my world though, there are only two types, power boats and sail boats. I'll keep most of my observations on sail boaters to myself, lest I piss off half my readers. Actually I've made many great sailing friends, so I'm semi-qualified to comment. First thing is this; most of them rarely sail. Oh they own a sailboat. It sits in a marina 360 days a year.

When they do manage to leave the slip, it's either not windy enough to put up the sails, too windy to put up the sails, or the wind is blowing in the wrong direction to put up the sails. They run their diesel just like me, but call me a stink potter. Silly rag haulers. (Or blow boaters, whichever you prefer.)

You heard these before; a boat is a hole in the water that you throw money into. BOAT stands for Break Out Another Thousand. Those are what you call "truisms" . . . because they are true.

Bilges are generally nasty places to be. Any work done down here is ten times harder than if you could actually reach or see what you're trying to fix.

It's really important to go down into the bilge occasionally to look around. Regular inspections can head off all sorts of emergencies. Don't ask me how I know that.

I prefer old boats to new ones. Old boats have style and grace. New boats are cheap whores. (My boat is old.) Some old boats are classics, like mine. Some old boats are just junk. New boats are lots of fluff and plastic. Some new boats are just junk.

Never, ever, ever own a wooden boat. You ain't got enough time and you ain't got enough money.

The Rule of Gross Tonnage: If you're the smaller boat, get the Hell out of the way.

Yes bananas are bad luck on a boat, (proven fact). Don't even bring Banana Boat sunscreen onto your vessel. Bullfrog brand works for me.

Boats steal things, or at least hide them from me. Every day I'll look for something and can't find it. Some things I never do find.

One engine or two? It's like having a woman. If you just have one and you treat her right, she'll treat you right.

Why do boats that never leave the marina have autopilots and radar and such?

It's always best to keep the water on the *outside* of the boat. Sooner or later though, water will find its way in. Fix that immediately, it will only get worse. Water always wins.

On a boat, especially an older one, things break. Just accept it as a fact of the boating life. Things that are supposed to move quit moving. Things that are supposed to stay still, come loose.

It's better to have improvisational skills like MacGyver, then it is to have spare parts for everything. Right now my dinghy outboard is being held together with a piece of duct tape and the body of a Bic pen.

Don't buy a boat with tons of teak. You'll soon learn to hate it, unless you let it go natural. Ask six boat owners the best way to care for teak. You will get six different answers.

Ask six different boat owners which anchor style is best. You'll get six different answers again.

Don't anchor near me with a loud Briggs & Stratton portable generator. If you have to go portable, buy a Honda, your neighbors will appreciate it.

My boat is a living entity. I talk to her nice. I treat her right. She returns the favor. When your vessel brings you safely out of a hairy situation, take a minute and pat her on the transom. Tell her she done good.

Renaming boats is okay **IF** you follow the proper procedure and ceremony. Boats that are renamed without proper ceremony sink ten times more often than those who been renamed properly, (proven fact.) Plus the ceremony is a good excuse to drink champagne.

Don't name your boat something stupid. I see this every day. No trite crap like Black Pearl or Serenity should ever see another transom. No unpronounceable names either. No French. Think about the day you need to call the Coast Guard. Can they understand what the hell your boat name is? Also rule out the words Reel, Sea and Knot. It's been done to death people.

Learn how to anchor properly before you embarrass yourself again.

Boat owners are a superstitious group. There are so many superstitions involving boats it's hard to remember them all. Try to follow them though, just in case. One exception; an old pirate superstition is that women on boats is bad luck. All of those pirates were either killed in battle or hung with a rope, so it didn't appear to work out for them. Women on boats is actually good luck, especially if they cook and clean.

A terrible skipper was going back and forth through the anchorage, searching for a place to drop the hook before dark. Looking up to heaven he said, "Lord take pity on me. If you find me a good spot, I will donate to charity, give up the demon rum, treat women with respect, pay my taxes, and never again give my crew all of the blame and none of the glory!"

Miraculously, the boat with the best spot in the bay began pulling up anchor to leave.

The skipper looked up again and said, "Never mind, I found one myself."

Signs You Live On A Boat

Compiled from various interweb locations and personal experience
Sleeping in a house makes you feel claustrophobic because there isn't a hatch overhead to look at the stars.

You know smaller is actually *sometimes* better.

You find yourself bleeding from random places at random times.

You and your girlfriend define "taking a break" as moving about six feet apart and looking in opposite directions.

You avoid telling people you live on a boat just so you don't have to explain to them how you shower... again.

You are obsessed with the humidity...indoors.

You think butter only comes soft.

All of your pots have removable handles.

When invited to dinner at someone's house you ask if you can have a shower.

When invited to dinner at someone's house you ask if you can do your laundry.

The doctor assumes your body covered in random bruises is a sign of physical abuse.

You are the only one who doesn't want to win the big screen TV at the charity raffle.

You think CSI is some sort of yacht club racing acronym.

Kids think you're the coolest person on earth.

When you don't like the neighborhood you just untie and move.

You are content knowing that sailing is code for boat repair in exotic places.

You can assemble a gourmet dinner using only one pot and a spork.

Doing laundry involves a net bag, a moving boat, and 50 feet of line.

You have to put up an umbrella inside.

When asked for a piece of scratch paper, you hand them 80 grit.

You truly don't want anything for Christmas that doesn't come in PDF form or install on a Kindle.

You only get seasick on land.

Cardboard boxes, wrappers, and packing foam are thrown away before anything goes to the boat.

You define a good anchorage as one where you can get WiFi.

A fifteen minute job always takes an hour and a half since you have to pull everything out of all the storage lockers to find the right part, then the right tool, then put it all back.

Your wallet contains more boat cards than business cards

You know what a boat card is.

When visiting ashore, you wake everybody at daylight screaming "We're aground" when you open your eyes and see trees.

You define an easy chore as one where you only had to pull out 3 tool bags.

You covet new solar panels more than a new car.

You can identify boats by the sound of their halyard slapping against their mast.

Removing things from the refrigerator is like playing Jenga.

You gave up high heels for flip flops

You've accidently put your life jacket on in a grocery store parking lot out of habit.

You walk in the rain all the way back to your boat, carrying a backpack, a load of laundry, groceries destined to fall out of their bag at any second... all while thinking how lucky you are.

Filling the water tanks is a full day's work.

The only thing you do religiously on Sundays is wonder what day it is.

The first thing you do after setting the hook is check to see who you know in the anchorage.

Cutting the grass means diving over the side.

You find a sea otter lounging in your cockpit when you get home.

You think the roof leaking a little is no big deal.

You wonder why it's always low tide when taking stuff on or off the boat.

A warm rum and coke won't turn your stomach.

When you try to sleep on land you find you can only sleep in a hammock after rocking it.

You understand and pay attention to the entire weather forecast.

You spend weekends sitting in your cockpit with a boat hook beside you, waiting to fend off the next rental boat operator.

You can heat your home with a Bic lighter.

Every time you consider buying something the main consideration is what you'll have to get rid of to make room for it.

When visiting ashore you catch yourself pumping the handle on a faucet.

You consider a three minute shower luxurious.

You covet your neighbor's oven more than his wife.

You measure the length of a shower in terms of quarters.

You now consider a freezer the ultimate luxury.

You have to strap a bag full of water to your boom, then wait a few hours before you can take a shower.

You've sincerely wondered if there are any companies that make triangular bed sheets.

You know that styrofoam was invented by Satan, duct tape by God.

When trying to register a new bank account or anything to do with government, their computer won't accept the fact that you don't have a residential address.

All of your neighbors have your cell phone number, but only call when they want a weather report or for you to check on their boat.

You realize previously asinine Jimmy Buffett songs have started to carry a deep philosophical significance.

You only bring out the clear plastic Dixie cups for fancy occasions.

You visit a friend's house and worry that everything on the shelves will come crashing down when the boat heels.

Getting the "heat" question for the 1,000th time drives you mad.

Trying to find someone to sail away with you isn't being romantic, it's practical.

Your first iPhone app was the Weather Channel.

Your second was Tides app.

Your homepage is the NOAA National Weather Service

You've spent mornings standing in your underwear on the deck of someone else's boat, adjusting halyards, lashing lines & freezing your ass off.

You have given up trying to defend your lifestyle and are content with smugly thinking.....they don't have a clue what they are missing.

You have a clue what any of this means.

Waterside dining is Ramen noodles and a can of beer.

Wearing clothes with holes in them is no big deal.

That mildew in the V-birth can wait a few more days.

You have a love/hate relationship with Teak.

You haven't showered in four days.

You use funnels, hoses, towels or tarps to collect rain water.

You get so good at improvising repairs, you think MacGyver was an amateur.

You are an expert on things your landlubber friends don't know exist; Like bottom paint and zincs.

You have never seen American Idol or Duck Dynasty.

The world stops for sunset.

You give names to Sea Gulls.

It's not a rain coat, its "foul weather gear".

Your entire shoe collection consists of one pair of flip flops and one pair of Deck shoes.

You must choose between owning a toaster oven or a microwave, no room for both, (and the ice maker ain't going nowhere).

You once spent eight dollars for a bag of ice from the Key West/Dry Tortugas ferry boat.

You once traded a case of warm beer for a dinghy load of fresh shrimp.

Your friends have called the Coast Guard because they haven't heard from you in several days. (True story)

You have bathed in salt water using dish detergent.

You covet your neighbor's dinghy more than you covet his wife.

You can judge the salinity of the water based on the rate of barnacle growth on your hull, a rare skill.

You own a dinghy named "Patches".

You consider watching novices anchoring as grand entertainment.

You can tie a Bowline with your eyes closed.

You know what a Bowline is.

You can lasso a piling on the first try every time.

You keep a mental scorecard on how many mooring balls you've missed.

You keep a mental scorecard on how many tools or other important items you've dropped overboard.

When driving a car you turn to Port or Starboard.

You visit a friend's home and tell them how nice their Galley is.

Then you ask, "Where's the head?"

You check NOAA for hurricanes every day, even when the weather is perfect.

Rum

Caution: Drinking rum aboard this vessel may be hazardous to your health. We don't have this warning posted on our boat, but I think we probably should.

You see, sometime after 6:00 p.m. my wife, the left-handed Irish bartender, pulls out a bottle of rum. You will be asked if you care to imbibe, politely. Some of those who partook soon fell on misfortune.

There was the one unfortunate gentleman who made it home safely after a night of "the one mores" only to fall flat on his face once inside his door. His distraught wife thought he may need an ambulance. Heart attack? Stroke? Seizure? Nope, he was just stone cold hammered.

There was the nice fellow from Colorado who gladly accepted his rum rations. Shot after shot went down. I warned him on several occasions that it would sneak up on him. No, no . . . pour me another round. Another round it is buddy! Sure was funny when he fell out of his dinghy on the way back to his boat.

The wife herself has been known to suffer a rum induced fall on occasion. On our boat that usually involves smashing your face into the fly bridge ladder or walking into a mast stay. Neither of these is pleasant. I haven't fallen down as much but I get to explain that no, I didn't punch her. I was asleep (drunk) at the time.

Once upon a time we embarked on history's most epic rum tasting tour. Our goal was to taste as many fine rums as we could, searching for the ultimate one. The rules were that we both had to agree that it was the best. This did not turn out to be a simple task. Neither of us much cared for the really deep dark rums no matter how much they cost. Those aged in whiskey barrels we soon learned to avoid. I don't like whiskey. We narrowed the search to light or clear rums, still no dice. Finally we stumbled onto a new one, Captain Morgan Lime Bite. Cheap, readily available and much preferred by us both. We had searched the world over and here it was right at home in the neighborhood liquor store. Try it, you'll like it.

The rum drink called a Painkiller is a gift from God. Not the Annapolis/Pussers version. That's crap. I'm talking about the BVI/Soggy Dollar Bar version. It's pure heaven, (and it kills pain), guaranteed.

My favorite singer/songwriter once told a wicked good rum tale. He was partying on some island, having arrived by float plane. As the party raged on late into the night, the group ran out of liquor. The pilot remembered a bottle of rum given to him by a passenger that was still stashed in the plane. He went to retrieve it and as he presented it to his buddies they saw that this rum was called Big Black Dick. They shrugged and proceeded to pass the bottle around. It was awful stuff, truly nasty. All Jim could say later was "I just can't get the taste of Big Black Dick out of my mouth. Moral? Not all rum is good.

"Time Flies When You're Having RUM"
Erik Voskamp

"Why is the Rum always gone?"
Jack Sparrow

"Best ideas come while sipping Rum"
Pavol Kazimir

The word rum is probably derived from the word "rumbullion," an archaic term for a big noise and/or uproar. Needless to say, this is a hard word to say when you've had a couple of rums, meaning the word was destined to be shortened. Before the word rum was coined, this molasses-based booze was called "Kill-Devil," a term that makes a lot more sense the morning after the bender undertaken with the cheapest Kill-Devil you could get your hands on.

Following the lead of their pirate foes, the British Royal Navy swapped their daily beer rations for a daily ration of a half-pint (quarter-litre) of 160 proof (80 per cent) alcohol in 1740. The rum was usually mixed with the daily lime rations the sailors (nicknamed limeys) had to wash down to fight scurvy. Makes you wonder how the British managed to accumulate an empire when all their sailors were several sheets to the wind.

If it be the design of Providence to extirpate these savages in order to make room for the cultivation of the earth, it seems not improbable that rum may be the appointed means.

~ Benjamin Franklin

Weather

When it rains your stuff gets wet. A boat is not a house. We do our best to keep the water on the outside of the boat, but water always wins.

Sometimes approaching rain means getting a bar of soap ready, especially for Nick. You'll meet him in the next chapter.

A nice steady rain is a good time to scrub the decks. A raging thunderstorm is not.

It's good for your trawler to be anchored near sailboats during frequent lightning. The taller mast will get struck first.

Keep your dinghy clean. If it fills up with rainwater you can bathe in it.

Soft puffy white clouds are not rainmakers. However, when you notice them developing vertically, that means rain is coming.

In the heat of summer in SW Florida, the cooler air off the Gulf moves inland in the afternoon. It collides with the much hotter air inland and creates those afternoon storms. They mostly miss the coastal areas all together. We sit and watch them form and explode 10 to 15 miles to our east.

That afternoon sea breeze is sometimes the only thing saving us from heat stroke. Well, that and the cold beer.

After several years living aboard with no air conditioning, we freeze to death going to the grocery store.

Wind blows.

I am not a sailor. I hate wind. Wind makes waves. Wind rocks your house. Wind blows your swim trunks overboard. Wind blows your favorite beer coozie overboard. (True stories)

Wind sucks.

In Florida, wind blows from the north during the winter. It comes from the south in summer, if at all. Choose anchorages accordingly.

The only good thing I can think of about wind is that it keeps the skeeters and No-See-Ums at bay. (Except in the Everglades, **nothing** stops those blood sucking bastards in the Everglades.)

Liveaboard boaters loose all sense of decorum when it's stinking hot. Blue tarps, beach towels, sheets, etc. all become shade makers. If you're burning up you'll hang anything anywhere if it provides you some relief. A really hot day with no breeze makes an anchorage look like its laundry day.

Maybe it's those really hot days that make boaters go naked. I'll ask Nick the next time I see him. (You'll meet Nick in the next chapter).

Winter in this part of Florida lasts for two days. It's usually in the first week of January.

Calendar winter in Florida means no rain, none whatsoever. It won't rain a drop for 3 or 4 months.

Summer in Florida means it will rain every single day. The Amazon Rainforest has nothing on south Florida in the summer time.

The Florida sun will turn a Yankee's skin red in two minutes flat. (Proven fact)

Hurricanes: Be where they ain't. As soon as the weatherman tells you where it's going to land, go there and ride it out. They never land exactly where predicted.

I don't recommend staying on a boat during a hurricane. Take every possible precaution to secure her, then go stay in a hotel. Spend the night praying she'll still be there in the morning.

2013 Hurricane season has passed without a single hurricane making landfall in the U.S. That could mean we're in a positive trend, or it could mean we are way overdue. How's that for weather prognosticating?

A man in a sailboat is adrift on the ocean when, suddenly, a fierce storm comes up. A man in a powerboat pulls up alongside the man and offers to tow him to safety. The man responds, "I am a devout man. I know that God will save me - you go ahead into shore." With this, the man in the powerboat roars away.

The storm gets worse. A Coast Guard patrol boat pulls up alongside the sailboat and offers to tow the man to safety. The man again responds, "I am a devout man. I know that God will save me - you go ahead into shore." With this, the Coast Guard leaves the man, his sailboat bobbing in the increasingly rough water.

The storm is really wild now - waves are splashing over the sailboat. A helicopter comes out of the sky, hovers over the sailboat, and a ladder drops down to the man. He waves them off, yelling to be heard over the roar of the wind, "I am a devout man. I know that God will save me!" With this, the helicopter flies away.

The storm rages out of control... the sailboat is overturned... the man is swept off the boat and drowns.

Being such a devout man, he immediately goes up to heaven.

Upon seeing God, the man says to Him, "I worshipped you all my life and I devoted my life to serving you, yet you didn't save me from the storm! WHY??"

God replied, "My son, though you were a devout man, you were pretty darned stupid! I tried to save you! I sent a powerboat, I sent the Coast Guard, I sent a helicopter..."

Nekkid People

I don't know what it is about boats and nudity. Maybe the feeling of freedom a boat provides leads to wanting to take your clothes off. Unfortunately, most of my encounters with nekkid people means catching two 80 year olds skinny dipping.

I hit my private beach one day and stumbled upon said 80 year olds naked. I expected them to scramble for their clothes as I averted my gaze. Nope. They didn't give a shit. They went about a normal beach day, sunning, swimming and reading, all sans clothes. It was a bit disturbing, mostly because I couldn't help but look, like a train wreck.

My best cruising buddy never wears clothes unless I make him. When I approach his boat I don't say "Ahoy", I say "Put some pants on damn it." He says it saves on doing laundry.

We've several times anchored near a boat named War Dept. Its captain is named Nick. My wife calls him Nick the Dick, because she's seen it so many times. He doesn't give a shit either. He showers on deck no matter who can see.

I have showered on deck naked, but only when no one else is around. Call me modest, it beats being called Nick the Dick.

My wife likes being naked. She runs around bare-assed all the time. When we come to a marina, I have to remind her that folks might get a clear view of her white hiney.

Willy T's in the BVI has a good scam going. They give the ladies a free T-shirt for jumping overboard topless. Good scam indeed.

I have never once in all my travels seen a really hot young babe walking around naked. Topless middle aged women I've seen. Eighty year old naked women I've seen.

Best naked chick viewing experience: One evening we dinghied over to our favorite sand bar for happy hour. There were two couples in the water up to their shoulders. As I passed by the ladies rose up to expose their bare breasts. Not bad, not hot young babes, but reasonably attractive. As the beer flowed and sunset approached we realized they were all completely nekkid. These gals were pushing 40 but they were fit enough. Finally they all boarded their boat, still nude, and made their departure. The two nekkid ladies embraced and kissed a long, slow, tongue exposing time. It was clearly staged for our benefit, which I didn't mind one bit.

Even as modest as I am, I've been naked out on deck many times. We shower outside a lot. The best time though was when we found ourselves all alone in a beautiful anchorage. With no other boats in sight we made love up on the bow. There was no one around to see us except the dolphins. They didn't seem to mind.

I wish Nick would shower inside his boat.

I hope I don't run into those 80 year olds again.

I wish I could visit Willy T's in the BVI again.

If you anchor near me and feel the urge to go nude, remember I've got binoculars.

We have our own private beach. We call it Sand Dollar Beach for obvious reasons. However, this is the spot where I've seen the most naked people. Maybe we should rename it Nude Beach. Or maybe we should get more creative. How about Swinging Dick Beach, or Saggy Boobs Beach? Tits, Pits, and Ass Beach? I supposed Clothing Optional Beach would be more appropriate.

Between the secluded beaches and boats at anchor, I've seem more naked people outdoors in the past few years, than in my entire life prior to living on a boat. If the quality of nakedness was higher, I'd call that a plus.

Trust me. You don't want to see Nick naked.

You probably don't want to see me naked either. Miss Kim on the other hand . . . .

I am blessed to see her nakedness every day.

Deflatables

This chapter is about dinghies. The dinghy is the most important accessory you can own if you live on a boat at anchor. It is your station wagon, mini-van, pickup truck and taxi. It is your grocery getter, water re-filler, trash remover and fishing vehicle.

There are lots of different types of dinghies. There's the plastic little rowboat type. There's the all fiberglass pontoon called a water tender. You've got fold-up boats, go-fast boats, putt-putt boats and everything in between. Just eyeball the dinghy dock in Key West Bight and you'll get the idea.

The most common type of dinghy is the Inflatable, but that is a horrible misnomer. These rubber blow-up boats should instead be called Deflatables. The best version is the RIB, which stands for rigid inflatable boat. I'm guessing the marketing people thought "limp, deflatable boat" wasn't catchy enough.

My personal dinghy saga: We just bought our trawler and had no dinghy. I found a fantastic deal. Dinghy and motor for 500 bucks. You can't beat that. Two days after I bought it, I noticed it was limp. I followed all the directions to apply a patch on a seam. The next day we found it leaking around the patch, so we patched it again, placing a patch on a patch. The next day we found another new leak further down the seam. Patched it. Next day same thing. Every time I patched one spot, a new leak would appear at the next weakest place on the seam. Eventually we had more patched area than non-patched area. Eventually we ran out of patches and glue and just gave in. This is the dinghy we named Patches. (side note:

had a friend who we teased constantly about having a rubber blow up girlfriend. We called her Patches)

We finally gave Patches away to a sailor in need. In exchange he cleaned our boat bottom several times. He still has old Patches. We visit her sometimes.

After Patches we bought a solid fiberglass dinghy that looks just like an inflatable. It was built by Boss Boats in Fort Myers. It looked so pretty and we figured this would solve our deflatable issues. No more patching and gluing, no more pumping up with air. We used the thing a few days before we decided we hated it. Don't ever buy one of these contraptions. It was slow, heavy and very wet. You couldn't go slowly across a millpond on a calm day without getting soaked.

We went back to the drawing board. We searched Craigslist until we found a likely replacement. We drove to Naples to purchase a ten foot Walker Bay RIB. Believe me. I checked it out thoroughly before plunking down my cash. It had no leaks! Imagine that! We proudly splashed it alongside our trawler and prepared for an extended stay away from the dock. We anchored out and enjoyed our new dinghy for three weeks. We loved it. Then on day 22, I awoke to a horrible sight. The new dinghy had joined the ranks of the Deflatables.

In the meantime, assorted accessories had started to fall off. I tried re-gluing them with little success. Nothing would stick. We named this dinghy Slick.

I've since managed to tame the massive blow-outs enough to render Slick usable. All the adhesive makes for an ugly boat, but what are you gonna do? We are stuck with Slick for now. Besides, beauty is in the eye of the dinghy holder.

Tits, Pits, and Ass

Tits, Pits, and Ass? What? If this was the game show Jeopardy, that would be the answer to "What is a whore-bath?" (Or for the men, "What is a G.I. shower?")

You see, next to monitoring the poop tank level, conserving water is the most important consideration aboard a boat at anchor. One does not simply take a shower every day. That would be a huge waste of precious water. So instead you get yourself a washcloth or wet wipe of some kind, and you hit the important spots. It's not exactly refreshing, but it helps combat the odor.

It's also important that both spouses maintain the same schedule when it comes to personal hygiene. If you both reek equally, you tend not to notice so much. I'm fairly certain that if the wife gets a shower and I do not, she will think that I stink.

Water conservation is in direct competition with the need to be clean. When we first started out we heated water by placing a five gallon jug in the sun all day. I rigged up a bucket with a hose fitting. We filled the bucket "upstairs" on the fly-bridge, ran a hose down to the lower level, and showered right there on deck. If it was chilly outside or we had neighbors in close proximity, we'd run the hose through a port hole into the shower compartment. If it was a cool cloudy day, we'd heat some water on the stove to add to the bucket. Between the two of us, we could take our minimum showers and use only three gallons. Get wet, lather up, rinse off.

Sometimes on hot sweaty days it's not even that much, just a quick rinse with fresh water.

Sometimes on beach days we carry a bottle of dish detergent. One can get a satisfactory bath in the Gulf of Mexico with a bottle of Joy. When you return to the boat (before Happy Hour, can't be late for that) you quickly rinse off with fresh water. Tada! Clean as a whistle.

Later in our travels, I added a huge poly water tank up on the fly-bridge. It sits up there all day and gathers warmth from the sun. We run that garden hose wherever we need it. We shower or rinse off, we wash dishes with it, etc.

If we really feel the need to live life on the edge of luxury, we'll fire up the generator, turn on the water heater and take a real shower in our head, (that's bathroom for you landlubbers).

The biggest treat we can give ourselves, is to grab a mooring ball at Fort Myers Beach, or Punta Gorda and take a *real* shower in the marina. I've been a week without a decent body cleaning, so when I get a real shower I want to finish up, get out, then get back in and do it all again.

You can judge the quality of a marina by the cleanliness and privacy of the bathrooms. (Proven fact)

Don't judge me. If you lived alone on a boat with just your spouse, far from civilization, with the need to conserve water . . . Your Tits, Pits, and Ass would smell as bad as mine.

Most full-time liveaboards simply don't bath that much. We have no one to impress, we need to save water, we are doing our part for the environment, etc.

(None of those things are true, we are just lazy.)

Recently a long time liveaboard came to our marina. He has been living at anchor, off the grid, for some time. I observed him taking a bath in the cockpit of his small sail boat. He was using a one gallon water jug, bathing in the way he had become accustom. He is in a marina with excellent shower facilities. I don't get it.

We once anchored near a guy for a week and watched him bathe every day. He climbed down his boarding ladder with a bottle of

Joy. It was like a ritual. Each day at the same approximate time he took a saltwater bath with dish detergent. Later we ran into him again in a different anchorage. From a distance I wasn't positive it was the same boat. I waited until the appointed time. When I saw him go down the ladder with his bottle of Joy I knew it was him.

If you are a girlie, girl, or feel the need to shower, shave and shine every day, living on a boat at anchor probably isn't for you.

Things I Love

(About Life Aboard)

I did a quick survey of some fellow liveaboards, asking them what aspect of life aboard they loved the most. Here is sampling of the replies:

Cindy Launderville said, "Knowing that I can leave and go anywhere at any time. Also love the peacefulness of the water, especially at night. It has a calming effect, a way to make your worries disappear, if only for a little while."

Joe Eisenhauer said, "Peace, Relaxation, Calm, Tranquility."

Karen Patrick said, "Makes you mindful of things you don't normally think about, just doing things differently, with intention."

Tim Little said, "I think I like the minimalist lifestyle the most. Everything has a purpose and a place . . . If it can do two jobs, all the better. You don't have closets full of stuff that you never use or even care about."

Steven Roberts said, "My own utility companies, and fully understanding them. Situation awareness. Forced efficiency.

Katrina Greenwood said, "The cruising community."

Al Felker said, "The cost of living plus ability to move, plus freedom, plus independence.

The common threads that I see are Peace, Freedom, Independence, and Self Sufficiency. Those are all the great reasons to live on a boat. That's the big picture. There are many smaller moments in the liveaboard life that help to make it all worthwhile.

Watching dolphins play or hunt is always a special time. The breath of dolphins is one of the things I love.

So is watching Pelicans diving on bait.

There is nothing like watching the sun set on the Gulf of Mexico or over Cayo Costa Island, or in Key West.

Sunrise with coffee in hand, from the deck of a boat, is a spiritual experience.

Not having to shave unless I feel like shaving is a bonus.

Clear blue water.

Falling asleep to the gentle rocking of the waves.

Feeling closer to Mother Ocean.

Silence. Calm. Peace. Serenity. Tranquility.

An ocean breeze on a summer afternoon.

A beach and a book.

An afternoon nap listening to water lapping at the hull.

Stars, constellations and the Milky Way at night.

A full moon reflecting on still waters.

Tarpon cruising in gin clear seas.

Time to think. Time to read. Time to do nothing at all.

Going slow, living slow, breathing slow.

The ability to pick up anchor and relocate at any time is indeed a positive aspect of living aboard a boat. Fussy neighbors? Move. Want a change of scenery? Move. Bored with your current scenery. Move. It really is that simple. Try that with your house, dirt dweller.

Want to be all alone in some private cove in paradise? No problem. Want to find some like-minded folks to socialize with? No problem.

Living a simpler life.

Less Stuff.

Fewer worries.

Less Stress.

Sunsets are enhanced when viewed from the deck of a boat, (proven fact).

I would also add not taking showers every day, drinking lots of booze, and generally doing whatever I please as positive aspects of life aboard.

Things I Hate

The number one thing I dislike about living on a boat is . . . . poop, (See chapter one).

I don't care too much for hauling poop, pumping poop, or smelling poop. A land based house has no such problem. Poop is the enemy.

A universal object of disdain amongst real boaters is the jet-ski. They will be highlighted in the next chapter.

High winds are especially hated. When it's windy at a normal house, one just goes inside, shuts the door behind them and locks out the wind. On a boat, the wind will cause my house to rock and roll. Loose objects tend to fly around. Drinks get spilled, and that is a mortal sin.

When you are driving a car and it gets real windy, it may be a slight inconvenience if any annoyance at all. When driving a boat, wind is **everything**. If it's too windy, it could be a matter of life and death. Even moderate winds may be the difference between going somewhere or staying put.

Wind makes fishing harder or impossible. Wind makes for uncomfortable dinghy rides. Wind can steal your swimming trunks. Wind can spill your drink. Wind is the enemy. Or was that poop? Oh hell, I don't like either of them.

Dinghy rides on windy days leaves one with "Dinghy Butt". This is condition of wet shorts that closely resembles have peed oneself.

I absolutely despise mosquitoes. I know, you think you have mosquitoes at your house. Unless your house is in the Everglades you don't know nothing about mosquitoes. Living on a boat in Florida often means anchoring in quiet, peaceful coves surrounded by mangroves. Guess what? Mosquitoes love mangroves! They also love human blood, especially at night. Ask me how I know that.

The absolute center of the mosquito universe has got be the Little Shark River on Florida's southwest coast. I spent a week there learning this fact first hand. I do not wish to relive that experience. Plan your trips in that area accordingly.

Other boats anchoring too close can be annoyance. Sometimes it can be a thing I hate. It depends on just how close.

The same goes for loud generators.

I hate mildew. Do you worry much about mildew in your land-based house? I didn't think so. On a boat it's a constant battle to stay ahead of mildew formation.

I hate bilge odors. Does your basement ever smell so bad it reaches your nose in the living room? I didn't think so. It can happen on a boat. Then you have to scrub the bilge. I hate scrubbing the bilge.

Does your house develop barnacles? I didn't think so. I hate barnacles. Don't ever attempt to scrape a barnacle off a hull with your finger. It will slice you open like a razor. Don't ask me how I know that.

Having close neighbors in a marina can be a pain in the ass.

Heavy rain is not a lot of fun on a boat.

People licking the icing off my cake really pisses me off.

Laundry Nazis are no fun to be around.

Barnacle encrusted anchor chains and mooring penants are not problems experienced by land lovers.

I don't much like large wakes from inconsiderate boaters, Everglades mosquitoes, poop, barnacles, bad weather, and mildew.

Other than that, I've run out of things about living on a boat that I hate. Mostly it's awesome.

S.P.O.R.E
(Stupid People On Rental Equipment)

(A song by John Reno)

Well they take the whole family down to the beach
    Looking for a little fun.
    Checking out all of those water sports
    Because at home they ain't got none.
    There's wave runners, Hobie cats and para-sails too
    They'll just about rent 'em to any yahoo.
    Just sign that waiver, say you won't sue
    And we'll get you on the water today.
    Take out your credit card and bend right over
    You're gonna need more than a four leaf clover.
    You probably wouldn't do it if you were sober
    I'll see you out on the bay.

Stupid people on rental equipment
    We all know them as S.P.O.R.E.
    There ought to be a law to tell the damn fools
    To keep their ass on the shore.
    Stupid people on rental equipment
    We all know them as S.P.O.R.E.
    There ought to be a law to tell the damn fools
    To keep their ass on the shore.
*Disclaimer: Lyrics may not be exact. That's how I remember the song as I sing it in my head, but you know how people screw up song lyrics all the time. Besides, I'm not real big on actual research.

The piece of rental equipment most likely to be operated by stupid people is the jet-ski. I took a very unscientific poll, jet-skis won by a wide margin. There are other forms of rental equipment though. Each type is subject to use by its own unique brand of stupid people.

Jet-ski operators are notoriously ignorant of the rules of the road, or rules of the water if you prefer. They ignore manatee zones, no wake zones, safe operating distances and every other single rule that is intended to regulate their behavior.

Every year there are 400,000,000 injuries due to jet-ski accidents. (That number may not be accurate. Remember what I said about research.)

There has never been a documented case of a MENSA member operating a jet-ski. Neither Albert Einstein nor Stephen Hawking has ever rented a jet-ski. (I'm pretty sure about that one.) Leonardo Da Vinci never rode a jet-ski, but I heard he was working on the invention of one at the time of his death. (The first documented case of death by jet-ski.)

Our next piece of rental equipment that leads to all sorts of mischief is the moped or scooter, especially in Key West. Combine mass quantities of alcohol with lack of experience, add in large crowds of other drunken people, and you have a recipe for certain collision. Again, I have not researched this, but Key West has to be the leading city for scooter accidents in the world.

I have a friend who once wrecked his rented scooter beyond repair while drunk in Key West. Being drunk, he thought it would be a good idea to hide it in the bushes and tell the scooter place that it was stolen. Scooter rental guy accepts this excuse like it's something that happens every day, which it probably does. Disclaimer: Unnamed friend in above story is not really stupid. Maybe this is a case of Drunken People on Rental Equipment.

That reminds me of a song by James (Sunny Jim) White. This guy gets busted running the only red light for 300 miles, on Grand Cayman, while drunk driving a stolen motor scooter, in search of the perfect chili dog. The moral of the story is never drive drunk on a stolen motor scooter, and always keep a spare chili dog on ice. I need a chili dog.

Our final entrant in the "rental equipment most likely to be operated by stupid people" contest is the boat. Here in Florida there are many outlets that specialize in finding stupid people to rent their boats.

I once watched a rental boat traveling at a high rate of speed slam head-on into a concrete piling. The piling won. This was in broad daylight.

Each season there are multiple incidents of stupid people pumping gas into the rod holders of their rental boat. This cracks me up every time.

People who rent boats are especially adept at running aground. This is also good for a laugh every time, especially if they are traveling at a high rate of speed.

We once encountered a boat load of women in rental boat near Boca Grande Pass. They were all sunburned and drunk. They were also lost. Being woman, they simply stopped and asked for directions.

Let's get back to jet-ski briefly. A quick google search will find plenty of news headlines detailing the stupidity of jet-ski operators. Jet-skis Collide / One Dead.

Jet-ski Rams Boat / Operator Dies. Jet-ski hits Sea Wall / Tragic Outcome. It seems to me that we should outlaw jet-skis. If it would save just one stupid person . . .

True Nautical Terms

It behooves any boat owner or anyone considering a boat purchase to become thoroughly familiar with the terminology associated with boating. Not only will it make you feel at ease discussing boats, it also serves to warn others that you are an individual to be reckoned with. Here are some definitions for the nautical terms you will undoubtedly encounter during your life as a boater. Take time to learn them now!

Aboard - A piece of lumber that may be used to repair your boat.

Aft - Acronym for Automatic Flotation Thing. The Coast Guard requires that you have a personal flotation device for each member on board; these are the ones that are *supposed* to inflate automatically when you hit the water (and you will) to prevent drowning.

Adrift - A method of moving across the water when nothing on your boat works. You normally do not have a lot of input as to where you are actually going, but you can get there.

Anchor - A mechanical device that is supposed to keep the boat in one place (see dragging). These devices are sometimes used to submerge expensive anchor lines and chain when used without proper termination at both ends of the anchor line.

Astern - A type of look. Your spouse gives you astern look when you attempt to buy things for your new boat.

Bilge - This is a storage area in the bottom of the boat for all the things you dropped and can not find. Also a mixing area for water, fuel and head output; making retrieval of said dropped items a real adventure.

Bilge pump - An electrical device designed to remove the charge from your batteries. These devices only operate properly when the boat is not taking on water.

Bow - This is what you do in front of your banker when you are asking for more money to spend on your boat. As your boat will surely cost much more than what you initially asked for, it is imperative that you learn how to do this quickly.

Bridge - Something you cross to get to the other side of a body of water when you do not have a boat available. Can also used for removing masts of sailing vessels if the bridge is low enough.

Buoy – A navigational aid indicating there is something worth noting somewhere close to the location of the buoy, possibly to one side or the other or below it.

Capsize - They ask you this when you go to buy a hat or baseball cap.

Chart - The nautical equivalent of a road map. One must use charts instead of road maps because road maps usually only show roads and there are usually none of those in the water and besides you couldn't drive your boat on one anyway unless you had it on a trailer in which case you would need a road map instead of a chart.

Cleat – A template used to practice knot tying that allows knots to easily slip off.

Cockpit – An area of a sailboat in which people sit in order to get wet.

Compass – A navigational aid that accurately points to the largest metal object on your boat.

Crew - This term refers to the people working on your boat. They are usually friends or acquaintances that do not find out about the "work" part of the ride until you are away from the dock. Crews have a high turnover rate, they normally will never want to see you again, let alone set foot on your boat.

Deck - This is what your spouse will do to you after discovering how much money you have spent on the boat without first obtaining permission.

Dock - A medical professional, not sure why the term shows up in a nautical dictionary.

Dragging - A method of moving about when the anchor is deployed (see anchor).

GPS - An electronic device that allows you to navigate out of sight of landmarks before the batteries expire.

Gunwale - (pronounced "gunnel") The part of a vessel near the side used for supporting one's midsection while one is engaged in the practice of heaving.

Hatch - A device similar in nature to a mousetrap, in that it will drop down on your head or hand without warning. Also an opening for admitting water into the boat.

Head1 - It is the part of your body that sits on top of your neck; you should not be buying a boat unless you already know this. Also useful for storing items like hats, sunglasses and such.

Head2 – The shipboard equivalent of a bathroom.

Heave - A shipboard method for eliminating lunch when seas become rough. This is best done in proximity of a gunwale.

Hull - A famous hockey player (Bobby).

Keel - A stopping device for your boat. It works by contacting the bottom of the water body you are in, thus inhibiting forward motion.

Keys - These items are used for opening locks and lockers aboard your boat, starting the engine and things of that nature. Keys can usually be found in the water beneath your boat. Also a place in Florida.

Lee - A famous Civil War general. Also meaning away from the wind.

Line – What you feed your spouse in order to obtain funding for additional boat-related purchases.

Mess – A term indicative of food, more indicative of the way shipboard galleys usually look.

No Wake Zone - An area of a waterway in which you are prohibited from waking people who may be sleeping.

Overboard - A term describing the final resting-place for anything expensive dropped while on board a boat.

PFD - Acronym for Personal Floatation Device. This is a multifunction device normally used as a cushion, packing material or sponge. The Coast Guard requires one for each person on board to ensure they have something soft to sit on in case standard seating is limited.

Port – This is what you drink when you are on the boat. Also the left side of the boat, also a place where boats congregate.

Propeller - A metal thing that looks like a fan and is attached to your motor. Propellers typically do not have the same number of blades they came with. The propeller is a dual-purpose item. It both propels your boat through the water and catches stray dock and rigging lines before they can harm wildlife.

Rudder - This is the device that steers your boat. The rudder is usually the first part of your boat to come off when you hit a rock.

Rock - These are devices used to remove rudders from boats. Also what your boat does just after you fill all your glasses to the brim with port.

Sailboat Race – Two or more sailboats headed in approximately the same direction.

Stern - The flat, back end of your vessel, included so you have a place to paint the name of your boat. This does not apply to Hans Christian and similar boats because they have points on both ends and you don't want to risk sounding incompetent when trying to determine which is which.

Through-the-hull fitting - A leak.

Topsides – The part of the boat that is not in the water. Also what you should not be caught looking at if you are a married male.

Voyage – Any boat journey long enough to require at least two separate uses of the Head2, not counting the one that occurs within 10 minutes of leaving the dock.

Wake - This event is part of a funeral and often confused with boating. Also what boaters participate in (their own) when they do not practice safe boating.

Wave – A unique feature of water that enables it to gain entry into your boat.

Yacht – When discussing boats, if the other is determined to be smaller than yours, it is then customary to refer to yours as a yacht.

*Reproduced from bostonboating.com

Zombies Can't Swim

I'm going to write an entire book on this topic someday, but for now I'll just hit the high points. Think about it. What better place to survive the Zombie Apocalypse than on a boat?

Zombies can't swim, proven fact.

Most cruising vessels are extremely self-sufficient. Large water holding tanks and rain collection systems will keep you hydrated while those silly landlubbers fight off Zombies in an attempt to get some water to drink.

Many liveaboard boats feature solar panels. Solar recharges batteries that operate lights, refrigeration, water pumps, electric heads (though not necessary), and the like. While those poor unfortunate dirt dwellers hunker down at night in fear for their lives, you'll be watching My Name Is Earl on DVD, eating popcorn and having a cold drink.

Add a wind generator or two to your anti-Zombie floating home and you can power anything a normal house might have. Between the sun and the wind you will always have power.

An onboard or portable generator will allow you to make ice, run a hair dryer, iron your clothes, watch TV, run a fan or air conditioning, etc. Your friends who didn't buy a boat will be filthy, thirsty scavengers. They will be fighting for their lives against the Zombies and living in a state of total disarray. You'll be neat and clean, sipping a cold beverage, freshly showered and entertained.

When the Zombie Apocalypse happens, the benefits of living on a boat will be amazingly numerous. Anchor out in deep enough water and watch the death and destruction from the safety of your vessel.

Zombies killed everyone in town? Pick up anchor and move to a new location.

Caught all the fish in your peaceful little harbor? Pick up anchor and move to a new harbor.

Tired of eating Redfish and Snook? Take that boat over to the other side of Florida and catch some Mahi-Mahi. Yea that's right. Fresh fish will become a staple of your diet after the Zombie Apocalypse. Mankind will be scavenging dumpsters and resorting to cannibalism. You'll be dining on fresh caught Grouper.

Let's say the ZA only happens in America. Simply sail to the Caribbean and ride it out. Your old neighbors will suffer through the worst catastrophe in the history of the world, while you sit on a white sand beach and take a nap.

Speaking of sailboats, if the ZA was so bad, like nuclear bad, one could last a long, long time far out to sea on a sailboat. With adequate provisions and plenty of fishing tackle, you could outlast the worst of the collapse of civilization. Ever seen the movie Waterworld?

Most cruising folks have become experts at long term provisioning. Storage of canned goods, conservation of water and other resources, clever meal preparation with the tools at hand, etc., are all old hat for liveaboard cruisers.

Prepping and living off the grid are all the rage these days. These folks are missing out on the obvious. Log cabins and secret caches of supplies are all fine and good until the Zombies find you. Knowing that Zombies can't swim, a boat will be the place to be.

A boat is mobile. Go where the Zombies ain't.

A boat can be self-sufficient. Loss of the power grid will not affect you.

After the Zombies and human survivors eat all the available food, you can still catch and eat fish. Find a Zombie-less island and maybe you can add coconut and sea grapes to the menu. Gopher Tortoises live on islands too. Turtle soup would be a nice change of pace. I know manatees are cute and all, but think how long one big fat sea cow would feed your family. Besides, I hear it tastes like chicken.

Trust me, I have a lot of experience living on a boat. How much experience do you have fighting Zombies? There is no doubt in my mind that during the Zombie Apocalypse, a boat will be the way to escape.

That's the best advice you will ever get, for only the price of this book.

The Tim Dorsey Chapter

For those of you who don't know who Tim Dorsey is, I urge you to pick up and read all of his books featuring Serge Storms. Tim is a New York Times bestselling author and Serge is a loveable serial killer. I asked Tim to contribute a chapter for this book. He told me that contractual obligations prevented him from participating in the project.

I wanted his input because most of what I see and write about takes place in Florida. No one knows more useless yet interesting trivia about Florida than Serge Storms. Tim would have been perfect, but it was not to be. What you're left with is the chapter that would have been written by Tim Dorsey, had he said yes.

When I first thought of contacting him, I wondered what sort of chapter would he write? What would the frenetic mind of a writer who makes you root for a psychopath think when presented with the topic of Poop, Booze, and Bikinis? Maybe something like this:

Poop, Booze, and Bikinis! Hot damn that's a catchy title! It's more than a book. It's a concept. I know . . . it's a movie. We'll film the ultimate Florida road trip. We hit all my favorite bars and beaches. Wait. We do it by boat, the ultimate Florida Dive Bar Bikini Cruise.

We start in Tampa. There's more poop floating in the rivers there than sand on the beach. Just this summer a sewage line rupture sent raw sewage flowing around houses on Spruce Street, in Tarpon Springs. Last year, in November 1.5 million gallons erupted into Sarasota Bay. In June 3.5 million gallons poured from a pipe leading to Bradenton. In March, 5.8 million gallons of poop burst from a pipe in Tampa. I can show you some poop.

No sense drinking booze there with all that sewage floating around. We'll head south a bit in your trawler to Charlotte Harbor. There's a lot less poop there. We can run that tub of yours all the way up the Peace River and anchor off the Navagator Grill near Lake Suzy. We dinghy in for No Panties Thursday and film all the drunks dancing on the bar and posing for pictures with giant panties. Old Florida will be at its quirkiest. No Panties Thursday is the best. Mostly locals instead of tourists like on the weekends. This place is so far out, when you drive away you have to dodge armadillos on Peace River Road. Leaving by boat you have to dodge alligators. Nancy in Saran wrap, Dennis in a Speedo, and Navagator Beer.

Where to next? Let's motor on to Matlacha and visit Bert's Bar and Grill. It's the ultimate dive bar with a million dollar view. It's right next to the "fishingest bridge in Florida". This place was made famous in a book called Pioneer Go Home, which later became an Elvis movie, called Follow That Dream. So many stories it could tell. The owner Bernard blends the locals with the tourists, fishermen in tank tops with dudes in flowered shirts, bikers and boaters, and mostly keeps the peace. You want funky? I give you Matlachee.

Less funk and more booze? Fire up the boat again. We're heading to Saint James City and the Low Key Tiki. On the way I'll show you what's left of the San Carlos Hotel. Thomas Edison, Henry Ford, Harvey Firestone, and President Theodore Roosevelt used to hang out there and go tarpon fishing. There was also a huge hemp farm and factory there in the early 1900s. The Low Key is a superb locals bar. Somehow the only other nearby drinking hole managed to piss off the locals who have boycotted it ever since. They congregate in earnest at the Low Key. We have to stop here when Gary and Kerri are performing. My God that girl has the voice of an angel. She should be famous, not singing to a group of expat locals on Pine Island.

This bar by boat tour could go on forever. First we stop off in Fort Myers Beach and sit at the Lani Kai. The hotel is a dump but it's superb in the bikini department. We swing it down thru the Keys and hit all the famous dives. I know them all. We work our way up to the mainland and then it's bikini time. South Beach is world famous bikini watching at its finest. We wear fake lifeguard suits and then we can use binoculars. What a scam. These chicks wear bikinis all over town. They don't even need no stinking beach. The Florida Room at the Delano is a good old piano bar. We'll see bikinis while we wait in line to get in.

While we are in Miami, I'll show you the Virginia Key Waste Treatment Plant. It's got a pipe that carries partially treated sewage under the city of Miami and out to sea. If we ever get a good hurricane here, the poop destruction will be epic. Biscayne Bay would be one big poop lagoon. It's a pooptastrophe waiting to happen. That would totally ruin our bikini watching. So we move on up the coast and ogle the college bikinis on spring break. We visit Lauderdale, Daytona, and all the way back and over to Panama City.

We'll film everything. We'll put that Girls Gone Wild dude out of business. Poop, Booze, and Bikinis will be bigger than Porky's. We'll have so much fun in the bars. We'll smell all that glorious poop. We've got time right? There are so many interesting, useless trivial places to see and film in between.

The Poop, Booze, and Bikinis Boat Tour will be monumental.

Okay so I'm no Tim Dorsey. If you are already a fan of his, I hope you appreciate what I tried to do here. I'm certain he could have put together something really amazing for this chapter. Besides, if I had his name on the cover I'd sell a million copies. It was a brilliant idea that just didn't pan out. I will say this for him though; he's not too much of a big shot to answer emails from fans. He has been very gracious each times he tells me no.

Go out and buy his books. You'll love them.

The Jimmy Buffett Chapter

I emailed Jimmy Buffett to ask him to write a chapter for this book. He didn't dignify my request with a response. I'm sure he's really busy though, so I'll let him off the hook.

Jimmy has written several books himself. I particularly enjoyed A Salty Piece of Land. The reason I thought he could contribute to Poop, Booze, and Bikinis is this; take a slow ride through any crowded anchorage and the majority of the boats will be playing a Jimmy Buffett tune.

Why Jimmy? Songs like Son of a Son of a Sailor, or A Pirate Looks at Forty, were written for the boater. They weren't for your average weekend boater either. They were conceived with the real cruiser in mind.

"Mother, mother Ocean
I have heard your call
I've wanted to sail upon your waters
Since I was three feet tall"

Jimmy sings songs that speak to the soul of all sailors. Even Cheeseburger In Paradise was written after a long, hard crossing to Tortola in the BVI. His CD collection Boats, Beaches, Bars, and Ballads is a must-have for any well provisioned liveaboard.

Discover Boating asked their members to vote for their favorite boating song. Pirate Looks at Forty took the top spot. Messing About in Boats polled their membership for the best sailing song.

Son of Son of a Sailor took that honor.

Southern Cross by Crosby, Stills, and Nash took second. Jimmy covers that song in every concert.

His newest CD, St. Somewhere, features a song called Something about a Boat.

Jimmy himself has owned a bunch of boats, both power and sail. He's certainly got the money for it. He sings about boats, drinking, beaches and generally having a good time. It's perfect boating music. I don't know how we can fit poop into a Jimmy Buffet chapter, but he's got the booze in the blender and plenty of coconut bras for bikini tops.

Then there are the Parrotheads. Folks who are fans of Jimmy Buffett are a special breed. They are a bunch of laid back happy people who party with a purpose. They raise money for all sorts of charities and generally spread goodwill throughout their communities. Parrotheads are almost always very nice people. Boaters are nice people too. Liveaboards and cruisers are very sociable. They are quick to make new friends and always ready to come to the aid of others. It's pretty obvious why the boating crowd would favor Jimmy's music.

A few more Buffett tunes for sailors/boaters:

Fins

A Salty Piece of Land

Barometer Soup

Tin Cup Chalice

Margaritaville

Back To The Island

Coast of Carolina

Coastal Confessions

Knee Deep

Boat Drinks (awesome combining boats and drinking)

The Weather is Here, Wish You Were Beautiful

Lovely Cruise

The list goes on. Many of his songs celebrate the nautical life. They also celebrate living life to the fullest, albeit with a little overindulgence from time to time. Sounds like a boater to me.

One Particular Harbor

I know I don't get there often enough
　　But God knows I surely try
　　It's a magic kind of medicine
　　That no doctor could prescribe
　　I used to rule my world from a payphone
　　And ships out on the sea
　　But now times are rough
　　And I've got too much stuff
　　Can't explain the likes of me
　　But there's this one particular harbor
　　So far but yet so near
　　Where I see the days as they slowly fade away
　　And finally disappear
　　But now I think about the good times
　　Down in the Caribbean sunshine
　　In my younger days I was so bad
　　Laughing about all the fun we had
　　I've seen enough to feel the world spin
　　Mixing different oceans meeting cousins
　　Listen to the drummers and the night sounds
　　Listen to the singers make the world go round
　　Lakes below the mountains
　　Flow into the sea
　　Like oils applied to the canvas
　　They permeate through me
　　And there's this one particular harbor
　　Sheltered from the wind

Where the children play on the shore each day
And all are safe within
Most mysterious calling harbor
So far but yet so near
I can see the day when my hair's full gray
And I finally disappear

Jimmy has been called the Patron Saint of St. Somewhere, the Patron Saint of Beach Bums, Patron Saint of Drunks, Patron Saint of Key West, Patron Saint of Margaritas, and the Patron Saint of Old Florida. All of those ideas are encompassed by the liveaboard lifestyle. The next time you're in a crowded anchorage or marina on a sunny day, listen to the songs. I bet you'll hear some Buffett. When you do, simply Breathe In, Breathe Out, Move On. Now you see why so many boating types listen to him.

Pirates

I have long wondered about the fascination with pirates, especially among boaters. Again, take a look at any crowded marina or anchorage. I bet you'll see some pirate flags.

Why is this so common? Who thinks it's a good idea to celebrate bloodthirsty killers and thieves? After much rumination on the topic of pirates, I've decided that sailors and cruisers see the pirate as some romantic notion of escape. After all, we quit our jobs and live on a boat in order to make our own escape from the stresses of normal society. The pirate may have been a scoundrel, but he was a free man. The pirate may have been demonized throughout history, but also slightly admired. He has broken away from conventional culture.

You can trace the origins of this pirate love affair back to 1883 when Robert Louis Stevenson coined the phrase "yo-ho-ho and a bottle of rum" in his adventurous tale Treasure Island. Then all those Errol Flynn movies in the thirties made pirates out to be chivalrous and good looking swashbucklers.

In days of old, when ships were bold
    Just like the men who sailed them
    And if they showed us disrespect
    We'd tie them up and flail them
    Often men of low degree
    And often men of steel

Who'd make you walk the plank alone
Or haul you 'round the keel
From Jolly Roger, by Adam Ant

During my childhood our local lore had Blackbeard himself cruising the coasts of the Delaware and Chesapeake Bays. Now that I'm in southwest Florida, our history is rich with tales of the famous Jose Gaspar, better known as Gasparilla.

Florida folklore tells us that several of our barrier islands were named by Gasparilla and his men. Of course there is Gasparilla Island itself, home to Boca Grande.

There is also Captiva Island, where females captives were kept as concubines.

The most infamous of these island would be Useppa. Gaspar captured a Spanish princess named Useppa. She constantly resisted his advances until he got so mad he killed her in a rage. He instantly regretted the deed and took her to an island and buried her himself. This forever tagged the island with the name Useppa.

Sanibel Island was said to be named by Gaspar's first mate, after his lover who he left back in Spain.

In modern times, the city of Tampa celebrates each year with the holding of the Gasparilla Pirate Festival. Over 400,000 pirate wannabes don costumes and parade through the streets in search of rum and booty.

So we are back to the sailor, the liveaboard boater, and the cruisers. We make our break from conformity. We drink lots of rum. We listen to Jimmy Buffett sing Pirate Looks at Forty. How can we not feel a kinship with the pirates of old?

The pirates of the Golden Age were the James Deans of the high seas, living fast and dying young. Their adventures shaped the pirate mythology that still lives on today, fascinating us with tales of excitement, danger and romance. Behind our modern day keyboards and steering wheels, it's easy to imagine a life without rules.

Even Mark Twain toyed with the idea of the pirate life in Life on the Mississippi.

"Now and then we hope that if we lived and were good, god would permit us to be pirates."

I just Googled "Pirate Festival 2014". I got 53 million hits.

I Googled "Why Pirates Are Cool" and got 14.8 million hits.

I Googled "Why Pirates Are Cooler Than Ninja" and got 43,900 hits.

According to Hollywood, pirates are sexy. Think Johnny Depp.

Pirates wenches are sexy too. Think Keira Knightly.

Finally, I think it all comes down to freedom. Pick any of the reasons why we think pirates are cool – the food, the rum, the booty, the sailing ships to exotic locales. It all comes down to a pirate thumbing his nose at the world. "I don't care what *you* say the rules are. I'll live my life free."

That, my dear reader, is why people quit their jobs and live on a boat.

The Beerfort Scale

Back in the day, sailors used a standard wind and wave measurement scale called the Beaufort Scale. In this modern age we have wind and wave measurements and predictions at the touch of our fingers on all sorts of electronic gadgets. A new and more useful scale is needed.

The old Beaufort Scale read something like this:

1 Winds Calm   Sea surface smooth and mirror like

2 Winds 1 – 3 Light air, small ripples, no foam

3 Winds 4 – 6   Small wavelets, no breaking

4 Winds 7 – 10 Gentle breeze, large wavelets, crests begin to break, scattered
Whitecaps

5 Winds 11 –16 Moderate breeze, waves 1 – 4 feet, numerous whitecaps

6 Winds 17 – 21 Fresh Breeze, waves 4 – 8 feet, many whitecaps, some spray

7 Winds 22 – 27 Strong Breeze, waves 8 – 13, whitecaps common, more spray

8 Winds 28 – 33 Near Gale, Sea heaps up, waves 13-19 ft, white foam streaks off
Breakers

9 Winds 34 – 40 Gale, Moderately high (18-25 ft) waves of greater length, edges
of crests begin to break into spindrift, foam blown in streaks

10 Winds 41 – 47 Strong Gale, High waves (23-32 ft), sea begins to roll, dense

   streaks of foam, spray may reduce visibility

11 Winds 48 – 55 Storm, Very high waves (29-41 ft) with overhanging crests, sea

   white with densely blown foam, heavy rolling, lowered visibility

12 Winds 56 – 63 Violent Storm, Exceptionally high (37-52 ft) waves, foam

   Patches cover sea, visibility more reduced

13 Winds 64 + Hurricane, Air filled with foam, waves over 45 ft, sea completely

   white with driving spray, visibility greatly reduced

Below you will find a much more useful barometer of current wind conditions.

The Beerfort Scale

0 The surface of your beer is smooth. Beer can be set down on the deck.

1 Small wavelets in your beer. Consider use of a cup holder.

2 Beer may be knocked over, must be held in your hand.

3 Empty bottles will roll around on the cockpit floor. Must be tossed overboard.

4 Haul case up on deck to limit maneuvering around boat.

5 Nobody can hold on to more than one beer at a time.

6 The case of beer slides around on cockpit floor. One person must be assigned to sit on it.

7 Bottles can still be opened by one person. Beginning of difficulty drinking without spilling.

8 Bottles must be held in two hands. Only experts can get the cap off by themselves.

9 Two people required to open bottles. Empties must be thrown to leeward only. Some teeth may be knocked loose.

10 The beer tends to foam out of the bottle. Very difficult to find mouth. Lips split and teeth fall out.

11 Beer is all foam. Impossible to drink. Temporary abstinence may be required.

*The Beerfort scale was adapted from a similar scale found on the website Latitudes 38. I've altered it to suit my purposes. I would suggest switching to canned beer to lessen the effects of wind.

Stupid Boat Names

Every year Boat US publishes its list of top ten boat names. If your boat name is on that list, it's a stupid name. The names on the list are all overused, hackneyed, clichéd and well . . . just plain stupid. By all means though, if you want to name your boat Black Pearl, or Aquaholic, go right ahead.

My absolute favorite stupid boat name is Miserable Bitch. I saw this sweet sport fisher in Lewes, Delaware bearing that name. I had to know. After the captain docked I asked him about the name. He said, "my wife said I could buy this boat, but only if I named it after her."

I've seen hundreds, maybe thousands of stupid boat names in my nautical career. I can't remember most of them so I turned to my friends at Messing About In Boats for a refresher course. Here's their list, from http://messingaboutinboats.typepad.com/

Appalling Puns
"Hot Ruddered Bum"
"Si yes da"
"L.L. Boat"
"Sail Bad The Sinner"
"Bow Down"
"Sexual Heeling"
"Ahoy Vey"
"Yacht Sea"
"Makin' Luff"
Financial

"A Crewed Interest"
"Myovadraft"
"The Loan Ranger"
"Colin's Tuition"

Medical
"Biopsea"
"Irritable Bow"
"Bow Movement"
"Sir Osis of the River"
"Vitamin Sea"
"Autopsea"
Sophomoric
"Breakin wind"
"Blow Me"
"Poopy Express"
"Master Baiter"
"My Assiss Dragon"
"Wet Dream"
"Norwegian Woody"
Questionable on a Sailboat
Seen on a Catamaran, "Double Penetration"
"Spank Me" (Raceboat. Imagine the T-Shirts)
"Cunning Stunts"
"Rumple IVskin"
Aquamorons
"Blue Vein Throbber"
"Four Play"
"Sea Clit"
"Seaduced Too"
"Hoosier Daddy"
"Dixie Normous" (they wish)

"Lucky Sperm "

"Show Me The Money"

"Floating Seamen"

"Nauti Lust"

"La-Sea"

Clever

"Maid of Plywood"

"DILLIGAFF" which stands for Do I look like I give a flying f....

"If it doesn't come when you call it, why name it

"Weazel" with a tender called "One Eye"

"Change Order" and the dinghy named: "original contract"

"WOFTAM" waste of f'n time and money!

"Miss America" (Nothing as embarrassing as calling into the race committee to get a slip and saying, Race Committee, this is Miss America" or having to wear the shirts!)

"Time and Money"

"Head First"

"Sea Cup" (Skippered by a woman)

"Runs With Scissors"

"Support the Right to Arm Bears "

Relationships

"Don't tell the wife" How about that on a Mayday? Mayday, Mayday, Don't tell the wife!

"Alternative Girlfriend"

"Mom's Mink"

"FUJIMO" - (F___ You Jane, I'm Moving Out ...)

"She Got the House"

"Pissed N Broke"

Obscure

"Dances with Sheep" (Kiwi Boat)

"The World's Largest Prairie Dog"

"Shoot Low They're Riding Chickens"

I am not making this up

There was a yacht at the Arun Yacht Club called "Passing Wind." About 10 miles to the west is the Looe Passage, around West Sussex. A crew member was hit by the boom, and the owner called out the coastguard. "What is your name and position?" "We are Passing Wind, in the Looe"

And a few more:
- a Little Nauti
- Adoryble *(On a Cape Dory Typhoon)*
- All Gulls and No Buoys
- All my Ex's
- Bad Atti-toad
- Bada-bing-bada boom *(another aquamoron)*
- Banker's Hours
- Bay Bay
- Baysic Necessity
- Beaverlicious *(hmm! interesting)*
- Beer Bait n 'Ammo
- Bezerker
- Better Knot
- Between the Sheets
- Big E Nuf
- Bikini Bottom
- Bimini Cricket
- Bite Me *(on a fishing boat)*
- Knotty Boys *(at least it wasn't knotty buoys)*
- Messing About
- Bottoms Up
- Boat-acious
- Buoys in the Hood
- Learning Curve *(written upside down on a sailboat)*
- Sea-duction
- Sea ya
- Loon-a-sea

- Cur-n-Sea
- SeaRenity
- Tip Sea
- Seanile
- X2Sea
- LegaSea
- Itza -Du-Zea
- Tax Seavation
- Slipless in Seattle
- Feelin Nauti (*I bet you are*)
- Nauti Girl
- Nauti & Nice
- Reel Nauti
- Nauti Nurses
- Gravyboat

Please people, a boat is not a billboard for advertising your stupidity. Imagine your boat has feelings. Still want to name it Beaverlicious? Imagine you need to call the Coast Guard. Still think Shoot Low Their Riding Chickens is a good boat name? Additionally, any name that includes Nauti, Knot, Reel, or Sea is stupid. Keep it simple, classy, and easy to say over the radio.

My friends mostly have proper names on their boats. I salute their good taste.

Ivory Star

Redemption

Georgian Blue

Crew Zen

Bay Dreamer

Days after finishing this chapter, a good friend and marina neighbor renamed his boat Knot-A-Care II. There's one in every bunch.

Brass Monkey

We've all heard the term "cold enough to freeze the balls off a brass monkey". Where does it come from? I thought I had it all figured out. Nautical lore couldn't be false could it?

I guess you'll have to decide for yourself.

CANNON BALLS: In the heyday of sailing ships, all war ships and many freighters carried iron cannons. Those cannons fired round iron cannon balls. It was necessary to keep a good supply near the cannon, but prevent them from rolling about the deck. The best storage method devised was a square based pyramid with one ball on top, resting on four resting on nine which rested on sixteen. Thus, a supply of thirty cannon balls could be stacked in a small area right next to the cannon. There was only one problem - how to prevent the bottom layer from sliding/rolling from under the others. The solution was a metal plate called a "Monkey," with sixteen round indentations. If this plate was made of iron, the iron balls would quickly rust to it. The solution to the rusting problem was to make "Brass Monkeys." Few landlubbers realize that brass contracts much more and much faster than iron when chilled. Consequently, when the temperature dropped too far, the brass indentations would shrink so much that the cannon balls would come right off the monkey. Thus, it was quite literally, "Cold enough to freeze the balls off a brass monkey!"

In an effort to debunk the 'brass monkeys' story, Ralph Ahseln of Gresham, OR, writes, "There are NO references to 'Brass Monkey' in any nautical reference book available today. There are no words even close to it. Therefore, assume it never existed as a nautical term. The device that held ammunition on board was most likely wooden, sometimes rope. A BRASS device would be unlikely to be placed on the decks of a fighting ship. Brass would have been a poor choice of materials. The 'holders' were called many things, primarily a 'shot garland', sometimes called a 'shot grommet'.

Which brings us to the real problem with the Brass Monkey story: Ammunition aboard those vessels was called either 'bombs' or 'shells' if they exploded, or 'shot' if they didn't explode. There was round shot, bar shot, chain shot, case shot, cross bar shot, langrel shot . . . So the old silly saying would have been 'It was cold enough to freeze the round shot off a wooden shot garland.' Kind of loses something in the translation, doesn't it?"

In an effort to debunk Ralph's debunking of the 'brass monkeys' story, Gregory Sherwood of s/v *Imi Loa* writes, "Page 43 of Robert McKenna's book *The Dictionary of Nautical Literacy* states:

Brass monkey, a metal frame laid on the deck of a ship to help contain the bottom layer of a stack of cannon balls. The phrase 'cold enough to freeze the balls off a brass monkey' meant that in extremely cold temperatures the brass frame shrank more than the iron cannon balls, and the stack would collapse.

Sorry Ralph!"

Bob Bell of *Andiamo* writes, "**From truth or fiction Web site:** According to the United States Navy Historical Center, this is a legend of the sea without historical justification. The center has researched this because of the questions it gets and says the term 'brass monkey' and a vulgar reference to the effect of cold on the monkey's extremities, appears to have originated in the book *Before the Mast* by C.A. Abbey. It was said that it was so cold that it would 'freeze the tail off a brass monkey.' The Navy says there is no evidence that the phrase had anything to do with ships or ships with cannon balls."

*Credit http://www.latitude38.com/wisdom

So there you have it. You've got the original tale, then the debunking. Then you have the debunking of the debunking and finally the debunking of the debunking of the debunking.

The Stories We Could Tell

When salty old sailors sit around and swap stories at a dockside bar, they don't
  talk about sitting on a beach or gently rocking while viewing a beautiful sunset.
  Instead they try to outdo each other with tales of near death experiences at the
  hands of an angry sea.

If you travel about in a boat long enough, you'll have your own stories to tell.
  Boat things break, bad weather surprises you, you make a bad decision, some
  how you're going to end up in a situation you wished you had avoided.
  Sometimes it's simply running aground in soft sand. Then you sit for hours
  heeled over at a sharp angle waiting for high tide and a tow boat. If you are lucky
  you can work yourself free without too much embarrassment.

I once watched a sail boat leave a protected anchorage and head straight for an

obvious sandbar. Sure enough, he plowed his keel onto the bar and came to an

abrupt stop. This now grounded sailor simply lowered his anchor into his dinghy,

drove back the way he had came and deployed the anchor. Then he used one of

his wenches to crank himself free. I watched him retrieve the anchor and motor

into deeper water. The whole un-grounding operation was very smooth and

obviously well practiced, leading me to believe he had done it several times

before. As he passed close by I shouted, "Nice way to start your day captain." He

responded, "Just rubbing the grass off my keel." I thought to myself that it would

have been a whole lot easier just not running aground in the first place.

Sometimes a learning experience can be a little more frightening. We left from

Punta Gorda one day for a leisurely trip down Charlotte Harbor to our home base

in Pelican Bay. The weather guessers were calling for a breezy afternoon, but no

small craft advisory. No big deal in a boat our size. We made it halfway when the

wind quite suddenly picked up to uncomfortable levels.

By the time I decided I was uncomfortable, the winds picked up to "We are going to die" levels. By now we were closer to our destination than the place we left so

we could only slog on. We got within three miles of safe haven when the winds

picked up to "No one will find your bodies" levels. My wife at this point was

cowering in the corner of the fly bridge, sitting on the floor because she couldn't

stand. She wanted me to call the Coast Guard. She asked if we were going to

make it. I said, "We shouldn't be out in this, but we'll be okay." Meanwhile I'm

having a serious struggle trying to hang on to the wheel, our forward progress is

all but stopped, and we are being thrashed about violently. The waves just built

higher and higher. We were getting splashed up on the fly bridge, a full fifteen

feet above the waterline.

Kim started to cry and buried herself in a game on the Ipad. I was using all my

might and agility to hang on and steer without falling. Occasionally we would get

knocked over on our side but we popped back up like a Weeble. Weebles wobble

but they don't fall down.

I decided to push the engine to gain a little speed and keep running for shelter.

We finally found the entrance to our protected bay and starting thanking God for

delivering us from a watery grave. After we gathered ourselves a bit, I sent

Kim down to turn on the breaker for our anchor windlass. She couldn't get in the

salon! Our refrigerator was lying across the settee table. Our stove was in the

floor. Assorted objects both broken and whole were strewn everywhere. The

inside of our beautiful boat was a complete disaster. We got a side door open and

made a path to the breaker switch.

To add insult to injury, as soon as we flipped the switch the windlass started

dumping chain overboard. Now we are in a narrow pass, anchor deploying, chain

dumping everywhere and basically screwed. I'm screaming to turn off the

windlass. Kim is about to cry again. Life is not good today.

Finally we worked out the windlass problem, found a spot and set our anchor.

Never has an "anchor down beer" tasted so good. Beer first, fix problems later.

Eventually I managed to put our house back together and we lived happily ever

after. Now we had our own story to tell at the dockside bars.

Good friends of ours were making an all night crossing from Key West back to

the mainland. Seas got rough. Suddenly they heard a noise from the bow, a bad

noise. Running forward they see that their anchor had broken free from the bow pulpit and jumped overboard. All the chain was deployed and the rode was

rapidly leaving the boat. As they grabbed at the rode to cleat it off, the boat

suddenly jerked to a hard stop, then turned around backwards. The rode had

wrapped up in the running gear. They were effectively anchored, from the stern,

in the dark, offshore in the Gulf of Mexico.

Each wave broke over the transom and filled the cockpit with water. There was

no safe way to go under and cut the line in the tossing seas. The captain radioed

the Coast Guard to advise them of the situation. He planned to ride it out until

morning and hope for calmer seas. The Coast Guard called each hour throughout

the night checking on them. Come morning, he was able to cut the rode, but did

not know how much was wrapped on what. They raised the sails and headed back

to Key West. Once near Key West, they got a tow into the mooring field where

they were able to assess the damage and make the boat ready for sea again.

They lived happily ever after and added their own story to the dockside chatter.

Another couple I know set off on their very first trip bound for the Bahamas.

Some bad weather was about but they were in no hurry and hunkered down for

storms in safe havens. Leaving Little Shark River they encountered more than they

wished for. Readers of Leap of Faith, Quit Your Job and Live on a Boat, you'll

remember our own ordeal inside Little Shark, and leaving there for the Keys.

Apparently their crossing of Florida Bay was even worse than ours. When they

arrived safely in Marathon, the wife called out for anyone to come pick her up

and get her off this damn boat

I can tell you now that they lived happily ever after and can tell a story with the

best of them at the dockside bar.

So all you dreamers out there, you worry that cruising is dangerous. It's not

always a walk in the park, but for every one story you hear about someone dying

aboard a boat, there are ten thousand stories about people who lived happily

ever after, in spite of their brush with danger. At least that's what it seems like at

the dockside bar.

It's Alive

Your boat is a living, breathing thing. Okay maybe it doesn't breath with lungs like you and I, but it's alive. Boats have personalities. They all have certain traits and idiosyncrasies that make them unique.

They also have a way of making you pay attention to them or to let you know who's boss from time to time. Maybe that's why we refer to them as females. Don't believe me? Live on one for a while and you'll find out.

They also like to play games with you. My boat thinks "Hide and Seek" is great fun. Any time you go to look for something that you haven't used in a while, you play seek because the boat has hidden whatever you are looking for. Storage is always a challenge on a boat so you've invented all sorts of clever ways to pack stuff away. What you haven't invented is a way to find those things when you need them.

Even everyday items disappear sometimes. I lost a pair of glasses once. These were prescription glasses that I absolutely can't live without. I set them on a table or counter before bed every night. I never misplace them. One morning they were gone. We tore the boat apart looking for them. We emptied every locker. We removed cushions. We retraced every step until every square inch had been searched. Those glasses were not on the boat. How does that happen? Maybe there was rum involved and those glasses are in Davey Jones Locker.

Other times you absolutely know that you have a certain item. Say you need some duct tape. Oh yeah, I have duct tape you think. Two hours later your boat is torn apart again but no duct tape has been found. The only way to be certain that it will reappear is to go buy another roll. I tried that with my glasses, but it didn't work. I'm guessing if I get Lasik surgery they will show up.

A boat will make sure you don't get too comfortable or complacent as well. Who hasn't been tripped by a cleat? A stubbed toe is just a little reminder that you don't live in a house. Other times some part of the boat will just jump out and damage some part of your body. These are known as boat bites.

Other times a boat will get downright vindictive. One night the wife and I over-served ourselves. The booze flowed fast and long until I passed out on the settee. I had left the generator running which is a no-no for us. She staggered out on deck to shut it down. I was awakened by the sound of her crashing down on the deck. I staggered after her. I found her bloody and confused but I know what happened. Our boat was telling her "Go to bed Kim. You're drunk."

I was on a friends boat a while back. They had just bought it, hadn't even taken it out for a sail yet. It was raining as his wife boarded. She put one foot on the companionway stairs and was immediately thrown into the air. She landed hard on her back, narrowly avoiding a blow to the head. That was their boat saying, "Welcome aboard bitch. Just letting you know who's boss."

The way to stay in your vessel's good graces is to meticulously maintain her. Shower her with attention and she will be nice to you. Neglect her and she will make you pay. Haven't checked your batteries in months? Something will corrode and cause something else to stop working. Haven't cleaned the V berth lately? Guess what it's covered in mildew.

Yes you must respect the fact that you are living on a boat, and that boat is a living thing. Forget that and you'll find yourself walking into a mast stay because you were drunk on deck.

Your living breathing boat demands attention to every system. Forget that and you'll find yourself adrift with no engine just when you need it most.

You must not neglect any small detail of your boats care. Forget that and you'll find a flooded bilge while thirty miles offshore.

Overlooking regular inspection is a bad idea. Get lazy and you'll find yourself without steering in a marina full of million dollar boats. (True story)

A boat is so very much like a woman. If you find a good one and treat her right, you will both be happy. Treat her poorly and she will quickly become a harsh mistress.

Even while underway, you must always remember that your boat has feelings. If you find yourself in rough weather, don't blame her. She won't steer a straight line when the waves are too tall, but that's not her fault. It's yours. Instead you must apologize for subjecting her to adverse conditions. She may decide to cooperate, or she may not. Try talking to her gently and kindly. Loud screams and curses will certainly make matters worse.

Never embarrass your vessel by being a dumbass. She is stately and proud. Running her aground or fouling your anchor rode in her prop will certainly damage your relationship.

Women are like boats: They require constant maintenance and attention, and they cost a lot of money. Men are more like buses. Another will eventually come along.

More reasons boats are like women:

They have sexy lines

They cost a fortune to run
They can be hard to start early in the morning
They can't read charts
They will leave you behind if you don't hang on to them
Sometimes they are tied up
It takes ages to apply their makeup
If you neglect them they can start to look a bit rough
They can bang you in the head if you don't duck in time

Weird Florida

In my first book I called Florida the "schizophrenic state". There is no doubt that weirdness abounds in the Sunshine State. As more and more miscreants migrate south, the crazy Florida headlines are multiplying at an alarming rate.

Below is a random sampling of news stories and headlines that can only happen in Florida. There are no boats involved, but poop and nudity are represented consistently. These are all real, taken from assorted media outlets. You can't make this stuff up.

The Chicken Church

A congregation in Florida is crying fowl after passersby realized that its church looks exactly like a chicken. God works in mysterious ways, but not this one, according to an employee at Church By The Sea in Madeira Beach. "We're not fond of it being called the 'Chicken Church,'" she said. "It's attracting people to us for all the wrong reasons. I don't think they're attracted to come in and worship, I think they're making fun of it." OK, but it looks like a chicken. Go Florida!

The Mother Daughter Porn Team

There's nothing more Florida than a mother-daughter porn team. At least, that's what we thought. The Sexxxtons have made headlines with their keeping-it-in-the-family way of life, but things got crazier this year when the Tampa-based duo announced that they're looking for a father-and-son team to get down to business with. As far as we know, that offer is still on the table.

The Skunk Ape

In the Pacific Northwest, they call him Bigfoot, or Sasquatch. In Florida, we call him the Skunk Ape. He's either the stinky cousin of the hairy legend, or he's just been hanging out in Sarasota County too long.

The Robot Butt

After years of research, scientists finally came up with the apex of Florida video games—the virtual prostate exam. OK, the robotic butt isn't for pleasure (or is it). Doctors can use it to train for their prostate exams without ever entering ... a hospital.

The Mermaid Who Was Barred From Swimming

Floridian Jenni Conti's mermaid name is "Eden Sirene." Normally, that'd be enough information for a Florida story. But no— Sirene was barred from swimming in a Fishhawk pool because of its "no-fin" policy. She was last heard saying, "I wanna be where the Miami are."

The Dog That Shot His Owner

Wow. Such Florida. So ouch. Very pain. A dog in Highlands County kicked his owner's loaded, .380 pistol and it discharged, firing a round into Gregory Lanier's leg. Lanier was fine. Man's best friend, indeed.

The Violent Naked Pooping Masturbator

This is a contender for Florida story of the decade. As we all know, in Florida there are violent people, naked people, poopers and masturbators —but rarely is one man the total package. Gregory Bruni is allegedly that package. He reportedly started on the roof of a North Fort Myers home, then defecated and masturbated inside. He was naked. Then, he pulled a big-screen TV off the wall, rubbed some of the family's clothes on his face, and avoided gunfire before police arrived.

The Tycoon Who Adopted His Girlfriend

Polo tycoon John Goodman called it getting his money right. A Florida court called it fraud. Goodman tried to adopt his girlfriend, Heather Hutchins, so some $16 million would be funneled to her, instead of the lawsuits he was embroiled in with his ex-wife. He probably should have focused more on his appeal to a 2010 conviction in which he drunkenly crashed into a 23-year-old in Wellington, sending the victim's car into a canal where he drowned.

The Men Who Left Their Kids For The Strip Club

If three's a trend, then Floridians really *really* like to leave their children alone while they party at the strip club.

Meet 25-year-old Jordan Caraway, our most recent alleged pole addict. The DeLand man is accused of leaving a 3-year-old child alone in his pickup truck at 1 a.m. Sunday, while he boozed inside Dixie's Gentlemen's Club.

Witnesses say he was inside for 30 minutes before an employee spotted the child and called sheriff's deputies. Caraway claimed he left another guy to watch the child, but the babysitter also apparently got wooed by Dixie's dancers, according to the Orlando Sentinel. He was reportedly inside the strip club, too.

Caraway was arrested and taken to Volusia County Branch Jail, but he's just a drop in the alleged bad dad bucket:

- There's Kenneth Rowe, 26, who was reportedly wasted when he walked into a Daytona Beach liquor store and asked the clerk to watch his baby boy. Then he allegedly went next door to the Shark Lounge for a lap dance or two.

- Elliut Gonzalez, a 38-year-old from Orlando, is accused of leaving his sleeping 7-year-old daughter inside a car while he visited the Diamond Club, according to the Orlando Sentinel.

- Former NFLer Monty Ray Grow allegedly left his 3-year-old daughter in the car, unattended, while he partied at Diamond Dolls in Clearwater. He was arrested on a child abuse charge. The child was uninjured.

- Strippers do it too! Brittany Roman, 21, allegedly left her little boy to walk around their hotel lobby while she danced at the Diamond Club in Orlando, the Sun Sentinel reports.

- Edith Aguilar-Cardona and Israel Rangel-Ortiz, both 25, left their kid in the car for about an hour while they opened Pandora's Box —the strip joint—in Palmetto, WTSP reports.

- Brandi Roman (no known relation to Brittany Roman) allegedly left two children under the age of 6 in her truck, as well as a can of malt liquor, while she watched strippers in Tampa.

- Edward Condry Jr., of Fort Myers, is accused of leaving his toddler alone in the car while hanging out at a strip club in Tampa. At about 2 a.m., a manager at the club heard crying coming from Condry's car. It was Condry's 1-year-old.

Maybe it's time for late-night daycare centers at strip clubs in Florida?

Some more of my favorite Florida headlines:

Man Accused Of Express Lane Assault At Walmart
Man Beats Friend To Death Over BBQ Techniques: Police
One Eyed Jack's Melee Ends In Taser Prong To The Eyeball
Woman Accuses Ex-Girlfriend Of Decapitating Sex Toys
Man Refuses Cuddles, Allegedly Gets Threatened With Knife
Couple Forced Teen To Drink Booze, Smoke Pot And Drive :
Florida Man Assaulted Wife With Turkey Neck: Cops
Bad Santa Robs Bank By Brandishing Wrapped Gift
Woman Stalked Neighborhood Duck Before Killing It: Cops
Man Allegedly Calls 911 When Neighbors Won't Drink With Him
Charlatan Sentenced For Ghastly Botched Butt Injections
Woman Calls 911 To Report Drunk People In Bar
One-Legged Naked Man Dies In Neighborhood Rampage
Man Attacks Mom's Boyfriend Over Missing Can Of Shrimp:
'NOT HOMELESS, NEED BOOBS': Woman Panhandles For Implants

<u>Grand Theft Chicken: Men Allegedly Steal, Ride 600-Pound Bird Statue</u>
<u>Man Caught Picking 'Shrooms With A Gator In His Backpack</u>
<u>Man Tackles Illegal Kangaroo In Florida Ditch</u>
<u>Man Says He Fled Crash Due To 'Bad' Chinese Food, Need To Poop: Cops</u>
<u>Man Attacked By Gator While Running From Cops</u>
<u>Man Named 'Worm' Chucks Romantic Rival's Moped Into Ocean: Cops</u>
<u>Man Allegedly Gets Naked To Prove He's A Monkey</u>
<u>Man Calls 911 80 Times for Pot, Burgers And Kool-Aid: Cops</u>
<u>Salad-Munching, Masturbating Burglar Takes Toy Chopper For Joy Ride: Cops</u>
<u>Officer, I'm On Acid - Will You Cut My Penis Off?</u>
<u>Woman Poops In Yard, Says She's On Her Way To See Obama: Cops</u>
<u>84-Year-Old Whips Out Pepper Spray In Bingo Showdown</u>
<u>Sword Fight Over Fake Pot Ends In Bloodshed</u>
<u>Woman With Bare Butt Accused Of Pummeling Ex-Boyfriend With Papayas</u>
<u>Man Who Had Sex With Donkey Back In The Slammer</u>
<u>Armed Would-Be Carjackers Foiled By Stick Shift</u>

Those are all actual headlines. I kid you not.

Why A Boat?

There are millions of boats and boat owners in the world today. What is our fascination with boats? I believe it's really our fascination with the water, especially the ocean.

Two-thirds of the Earth's surface is covered in water. If you believe in evolution, all life evolved first from the sea. If you believe in the Bible, God first destroyed the Earth with a great flood, and we are all descendants of Noah and his crew. Noah's journey was the first documented incident of a sailor running his ship aground, by the way.

Even the human body is comprised mostly of water. That water is salty, saline like the ocean. Our very being is the same element that makes up the oceans of the world.

It's clear that we all have some innate longing to return to the sea. All of the countries of the world were discovered by brave men in sailing ships. The early Vikings, Columbus, Ponce De Leon, Magellan, and all those great seafaring explorers told tales of looking for gold, the fountain of youth, spices or other treasures. The truth is they just needed an excuse to mess about the ocean on a boat.

Today we either go to the beach or we buy our own boat. We post on Facebook how the beach is in our soul, or saltwater is the cure for everything. The beach is consistent. It is sand and water. Some beaches are prettier than others, but the general makeup is the same.

Boats on the other hand, are as varied as the people who own them. They range from the canoe to the mega-yacht. There are almost an infinite number of styles and designs. It may be called a fishing boat, a picnic boat, a work boat, a go-fast boat, a motor yacht, a kayak, or a sailboat. You may claim to want to fish, to work, to sail, to paddle, or to party. The real reason you own that boat is to be on the water.

The water is in your soul.

We are all children of the sea whether we know it or not. We lost our gills somewhere along the way, and our fins are barely serviceable these days, but our heritage is the sea.

It is the last frontier on our planet. It is the great unknown. It can be calm and peaceful, regenerating our souls like only the sea can. It can angry and deadly, taking lives and property with equal abandon.

We are drawn to it. It pulls us to its shores. It calls us to sail on her waves.

That's why we are boaters, and boaters are all kin. I'd like to say I love all boats and all boaters, but those go-fast guys piss me off. They don't know why they are drawn to the sea. They are loud and obnoxious and their women all have fake boobs. Cigarette Boats, Donzis and their ilk, we call them penis extensions. Still, they are drawn to sea.

The blow boater may confuse you with their fancy terminology, their fancier clothes, and their purist ways, but they are your kin too. They are drawn to the sea.

The commercial fishermen may reek of fish, have calloused hands and weathered skin, but he's not really after the fish. He is simply drawn to the sea. He is your kin.

The recreational fishermen may have more money in tackle than you do in your boat. He may talk about all the latest gizmos, his latest conquests and brag about his expertise, but he isn't really after the fish either. He longs to be on the water.

Folks paddling kayaks, canoes, and standup paddleboards are your kin too.

Even that rich bastard on the million dollar yacht is your kin, though you probably won't be in his will. He loves the sea. He wants to be on the water.

Those of us who own boats can't help it. We have heard her call. We've wanted to sail upon her waters since we were three feet tall. Our boats are the vehicle through which we worship her. They take us home. Our boats take us back to our origins, and our birth.

Yet there are some people who don't care for boats. I feel sorry for them. Maybe they are inner-city dwellers, or farmers with a deep connection to the land. For whatever reason, they have not heard the call of Mother Ocean.

Honestly, I can't see how such a person can be complete. It is my true belief that we need the sea to nourish our souls. Maybe true land lovers are more evolved than us sea lovers? Maybe we are closer to our roots.

Boats can make us one with the sea. We own boats precisely because we have heard the call. We need to answer.

We haul our poop, we battle mosquitoes, we crawl around in the bilge and we drink too much booze. We bust our knuckles and we bang our knees. We risk life and limb in bad weather. We pay for bottom paint, electronics and fuel. We live in a cramped space that rocks and rolls. We drop shit overboard. We go without a bath. We cuss limp dinghies. We freeze in the winter and we roast in the summer. We fight off mold and mildew. We scrape barnacles.

We wouldn't change a thing. Why?

We are drawn to the sea. We are all drawn to the sea and we are all kin. I salute all of you. I lift a toast to all the boaters out there, (except those go-fast guys, they still piss me off.)

Disclaimers and Acknowledgements

If you enjoyed this book, **please write a review at Amazon.com**. Reviews are very helpful to an author and are greatly appreciated. Thanks in advance.

*Every time I used the words "proven fact", the statement is not necessarily a proven fact.

*Every time I used the words "true story", I was indeed referring to real events.

Credit for the awesome cover goes to **KOI Designs Solutions**. It looks exactly how I conceived it in my mind. Image via Shutterstock.

Special thanks go to **Draft2Digital** for their excellence in formatting and publishing assistance.

Connect with Ed Robinson at: https://www.facebook.com/quityourjobandliveonaboat
Follow his blog at:
http://quityourjobandliveonaboat.wordpress.com/

Keep reading for a sample of my first book, Leap of Faith / Quit Your Job and Live on a Boat.

Praise for Leap of Faith / Quit Your Job and Live on a Boat

This is a wonderful story about a dream, determination, discipline, and courage. It's a gaze into the rat race tunnel, but it points the way out. Many will identify with it and take away something valuable. The author's narrative on life in the sun and sand and sea is mesmerizing. I loved this book.

Paul Carr, author of *The Cayman Switch* and *Long Way Down*

Just finished Ed Robinson's book (Leap of Faith) on chucking it all and heading off on a boat. Honest truth: I usually HATE any "look-at-me-livin-the-life" yarn but Ed is a gifted writer and offers an intelligent perspective on the process of getting out from under the hypnotic spell, and subsequent debt, of consumerism ... then having (just) enough to be enough ... and finally winning the freedom and lifestyle that ascetic living can offer anyone. Good one on ya Ed!

Mark Doyle, author of *On The Water Chart Guides* and *Cruise Guide for the Intercoastal Waterway*.

To be honest, Ed hit the nail on the head so hard in chapter 7, "Debt Free Equals Freedom" and chapter 8, "Save, Save, Save". I recommended everyone in the USA to buy this book and read it if for nothing else, these two chapters. If you follow Ed's brilliant advice, your life will be forever changed and all for the better. The book clearly lays out how ANYONE can get out of debt and live with forever freedom. This was a great read and I think it is awesome that this couple changed their lives so positively by doing just some simple adjustments in how they live their life.

Jim Baugh
Jim Baugh Outdoors TV
Author of *HOOKED*

Dreaming of getting a boat and living on it? Wondering how people who aren't millionaires manage to do it? This book lays it out for you. I enjoyed reading it. If you're just starting to explore the dream of heading off into the sunset on a boat, it's a nice roadmap of the nuts and bolts of how to actually make it happen. Ed Robinson was formerly a professional writer and the book is well written.

Carolyn Shearlock, owner *of theboatgalley.com* and author of *The Boat Galley Cookbook.*

'Leap of Faith' is Robinson's story—his journey from being an Everyman to someone who lives the good life. Surprisingly, his story is very much like everyone else's—that is, that part when he was still working his way in the so-called rat race, asking the same questions most of us could only ask in silence: what else is out there? But unlike most of us, Robinson actually had the liver to go from idle dreaming to actually finding fruition to his plans.

This book is his story—as well as those of the fortunate ones he has met along the way.

Spiritually, you can roughly categorize 'Leap of Faith' as an inspiring book of sorts—it can teach you about having some personal financial management, or how to really make crucial life-defining decisions. But at its most basic, the book can serve as your "rough guide"—you can forge your own path, you don't even have to buy your own boat, but the lesson is there—you can live the good life, and there is a method.

What's more, Robinson's writing is thoroughly enjoyable—he has a knack for telling stories from an entertaining perspective. There are people who tell stories, then there are those (like Robinson) who make even ordinary stories come alive and seem to jump out of the page. If Robinson writes a fiction novel, I'm sure it will be as immensely entertaining.

Overall, 'Leap of Faith' is one of those books, like 'The Little Prince', that you'll be instantly recommending to friends or people when asked "what life-changing books can you recommend?" This is one of the best, most inspiring books I have read in recent years. A resounding five stars!

New York Book Pundit

This book is the antithesis of "He who dies with the most toys, wins" Heaven knows I'm on that side of the fence, having spent my life buying the newest car, newest gadget and paying off three wives. Not that I might do it all over again, but I'm sitting at my desk working this morning while Ed is preparing his morning cup of coffee and watching the sunrise. If I can ever call something a "Must Read" Leap of Faith is it. Great job!

Wayne Gales, author of Treasure Key, and Key West Camouflage

Escapism at its best. This book is a must read for everyone sitting on their ass at a desk all day long, or suffering in life-sucking big city commutes, or simply wanting off the hamster wheel.

Jon Breakfield, author of Key West, A Pinch of Salt and a Quirky Slice of America

Ed shares his tips on how people can save and escape the rat race. His goal is to motivate anyone who has thought about chucking it all, realize that they too, can make it happen. My family escaped the rat race and moved to Belize, and I can relate to Ed's description of slowing down, and living in the moment. A book for anyone who needs a kick in the rear to make their dreams become a reality.

Sonia Marsh, author of Freeways to Flip Flops and My Gutsy Story Anthology

They say one of the signs of a good book is dreading to begin the last chapter, and this was certainly true of Leap of Faith. I didn't want it to end. My only hope is that Ed is keeping a diary because I want more. I would like nothing more than to continue reading about the adventures of Ed and Kim living aboard their Boat, The Leap of Faith.

Rodney Riesel, author of Ocean Floors and Sleeping Dogs Lie

Leap of Faith

Quit Your Job And Live On A Boat

(Available at Amazon.com)

There are many of us who dream about selling all our stuff, quitting our jobs, and

running away to Paradise. This is a story about one couple who made that dream

come true. The author shares what it feels like to experience ultimate freedom,

and outlines the steps they took to get there. The story includes tales from their

travels, social commentary on the state of today's American society, and a simple

financial plan that will benefit anyone, regardless of their future goals.

Throughout the narrative the reader is treated to dolphins and manatees,

pelicans and osprey, blue skies, blue water and white sand beaches. Tropical

music plays a role as well. Read how music inspired them to execute their plan.

Follow along as they transform from everyday working drones to carefree boat
    bums and beachcombers. This book will make you rethink how you look at life,
    and money.

Keep reading to sample Leap of Faith, by Ed Robinson.

I live the greatest life that's ever been lived.

There is a song by the Zac Brown Band where Jimmy Buffett himself sings, "Wrote a note said be back in a minute. Bought a boat and I sailed off in it." Well, I did just that. Now I am the happiest person on the face of the earth.

If there is anyone who can truly claim to live the life that Jimmy sings about, it is me. You can too. I have a story to tell, from nuts and bolts to anecdotes. The how-tos and the why-fors of achieving a dream life are in these pages.

Come on along. Enjoy the ride.

The Good Life

What's so great about living on a boat? What's so special about my life in particular you ask? Let's consider a typical day in the life of the happiest guy in the world.

As I write, I'm sitting on the back of my yacht. The boat is anchored in a slice of Eden known as Pelican Bay. She's nestled snugly between the beautiful island of Cayo Costa and the patch of sand and mangroves named Punta Blanca Island. The sun is shining in an impossibly crystal blue sky. Its eighty-four degrees, the water is flat and clear, and I just cracked open an ice cold beer.

I've got my feet propped up on the transom. It's time to reflect on my day. It's Happy Hour, after five but before sunset.

Before dawn this morning, I took my coffee in this same spot, same pose as a

matter of fact. There was just enough light to make out the dolphins nearby

hunting for breakfast. Those I didn't see I could still hear each time they surfaced

for air. It was still, peaceful and quiet. The lack of noise is profound.

No cars, no trucks, no sirens, no backing trash trucks going beep, beep, beep. None of the sounds that dirt dwellers become accustomed to are heard here. They are replaced by the breath of dolphins. I can here ospreys chirping from the island. Occasionally there's a splash from a pelican diving on bait.

That reminds me of another song by my favorite singer/songwriter Jim Morris. "Pelicans diving crashing on bait, pretty soon the dolphins arrive. I move down the shoreline and hear a snook pop, oh the mangroves are coming alive." Those are the sounds I hear.

Eventually the sun peaks its head over the eastern horizon. I snap a picture to share with my Facebook following. Lots of them tell me they would never see a sunrise if not for my pictures. Most mornings after I catch a spectacular sunrise, I'll head off in the dinghy in search of redfish, snook, tarpon, trout, grouper, cobia, snapper or whatever I can find. Fishing gives me great joy. Legal fish that are good to eat may become tonight's dinner, but it also keeps me in close proximity to nature's beauty that is all around me. I may see more dolphin, or manatees, or rolling tarpon. I may sit and float and just take it all in, letting the breeze take me wherever it wants to go.

On these quiet mornings, I could be lost in concentration trying to sneak up on a wily fish in shallow water. The world is blocked out. It's just me, my spinning rod and the fish. Or I could be totally aware of my surroundings, my eyes awake to every aspect of flora and fauna in this special place.

Afternoons I spend with my beautiful wife. She's a tall, thin blonde who at age
forty-seven still looks great in a bikini. After a late breakfast or early lunch we
head off to the beach together. It's not just any beach. It's white sand and clear
blue water. More importantly, it's empty of other people. It seems impossible
that such a heavenly place isn't overrun with tourists, especially in Florida, but
here it is. We have our very own private beach. Okay so there are a few tourists
about three miles away. They get dropped off by ferry boats near the north end,
but we never see them here. On weekends, we occasionally encounter locals in

their own boats who anchor near shore. On even more rare occasions we'll meet

folks like us. I guess there are few cruisers who know about this secluded beach,

but very few. Most of the time there is no one here but the two of us.

Our beach routine varies, but it always begins with a moment of standing and staring. It's so beautiful here, like a postcard. This beach is as nice as any in the Caribbean, and it's all ours. We look north at white sand with no sign of another human. We look south and can just make out North Captiva Island. We see the calm blue Gulf of Mexico stretching out to the horizon.

We set up our beach chairs, admire each other's ridiculously deep tan and just smile. Some days we walk. Some days we hunt for sea shells. I've developed a knack for finding sand dollars. The lovely Miss Kim is always the first to find starfish. Some days we just sit and read. Some days I'll fish a little off the beach. Whenever I'm out here with a fishing rod, I can hear Jim Morris singing in my head. "The Cayo Costa is quiet this morning. It's so good to be back on my turf. I walk through the sand, fly rod in hand, just looking for snook in the surf." Every day we are back on the boat by five o'clock, because that's Happy Hour. We shower up if it's necessary. I grab a cold beer, Kim fills a tumbler with box-o-wine, then we clink can to plastic and make a toast to another day in paradise. Later on we'll have some nips of rum.

Then it's time for the sunset. We celebrate it, each and every night. It's an important ritual all across Florida that you'll read more about later. Somewhere in there we eat dinner, but it's usually an afterthought, just sustenance. Some nights after dark we get naked and have mad monkey sex. Other nights we get naked and make sweet gentle love. Every night we sleep the sleep of the contented.

That's what it's like to be me. Can you see how I feel justified in claiming to live the greatest life that's ever been lived?

Smiling Out Loud

Some folks say I like to live my life like a Jimmy Buffett song. I actually prefer to say I like to live my life like a Jim Morris song. Here's a little bit of one:

He moved down from Long Island

He's living out in Pelican Bay

He's got a spot right on the water

He's got no rent to pay.

He's got no fussy neighbors

No gate no security guards

He fishes from his front porch

He's got the beach in his back yard.

It always seemed like a good idea

Buy a little houseboat free and clear

Living on Shrimp and Navagator Beer

Every day goes by without a cloud

And every time you see him

He's smiling out loud.

Yep, that's me. I listened to the songs and now I live them. But how did I get here? It all started with Travis McGee over twenty years ago. Prolific author John D. MacDonald wrote twenty-one books starring the tough guy hero. Travis always killed the bad guys and slept with the pretty women. I read all of them and he was my personal hero for several reasons.

In addition to his action filled exploits, Travis lived on a fifty-two foot barge type houseboat called the Busted Flush. He won it in a poker game and tied it up in slip F-18, Bahia Mar Marina in Fort Lauderdale. He went fishing often and admired the fish he caught, occasionally keeping one for dinner but more often releasing them. He mourned the loss of Old Florida, hating the development and draining of the swamps. He also despised the greed and corruption of said developers and politicians. He stood up for what was right. He helped those in need.

All that sounded pretty awesome to me, but there was one thing that intrigued me about Travis. He was taking his retirement in installments. He only took a case when the money ran low, or if he got guilted into helping someone (usually a sexy babe). In between jobs he lived a sweet life. He was a beach bum, a fisherman, a drinker but not a drunk. I wanted to be just like him.

It took many long years for me to figure out how, but as of today I haven't worked in over two and a half years. I've been living a life of leisure in a warm and sunny place. I'm a beach bum, a fisherman, a drinker but not a drunk. I've still got a little money in the bank. I'm only fifty years old.

Could you go thirty months or more without a paycheck and survive with cash to spare? I know that you think you can't, that it's impossible. You are wrong. You can do it. Maybe not right now, but eventually you can.

We'll get to that soon enough.

Who is Jim Morris?

At this point I figure there are some readers thinking, who the hell is Jim Morris? Why is he important to this story? Well, Jim and his music are essential to telling my tale.

Six or seven years ago, a friend handed me two CDs. He said he thought I might like the guy. I loved the songs. I bought a few more and they became all I listened to. It's a slice of the island life. It's quitting your job and running away music. It's clear blue water and a quart of rum. It's fishing and sailing and white sand beaches with a big ole jug of sangria wine.

Some guy I'd never heard of was changing my life with his music so I checked him out further. He tours the country some but is very popular in Florida. In one song he tags himself as a semi-significant star. I discovered that he and his band played nearby occasionally on the East Coast swing. One cold January day we made our way to the Jetty Dock Bar on Maryland's eastern shore for our first taste of Jim Morris and The Big Bamboo Band. I was surprised by the huge crowd and their enthusiasm. It was like nothing I'd ever seen before. My wife and I were both hooked. It was more fun than a Jimmy Buffett concert, if that's possible.

We saw them play a few more times and eventually graduated from Parrotheads to Bocanuts, as his fans are called. Kim and I were engaged at the time, and I came up with a brilliant plan for our wedding. I contacted Jim and asked if we could marry on his stage when he returned to the Jetty. He agreed and I made the arrangements. When the day came we had not only our friends and family present, but also a few hundred strangers.

The crowd started growing

The place started swinging

The beer started flowing

Everybody started singing

(From Navagator Afternoon, by Jim Morris)

It was like having the reception before the wedding, then a huge party afterwards. Jim was so gracious to allow it. The staff at The Jetty was very accommodating. Miss Kim was so beautiful. I couldn't dream of a better way to begin our new life together. I had no idea at the time, but it would only get better. I also didn't know how much more of a role Jim would play in shaping our future.

For our first vacation as a married couple we chose Punta Gorda, Florida. Jim holds his own music festival there annually. We arrived early so we could do the tourist thing before it began. We hit Sanibel, Boca Grande, and Fisherman's Village. We even rented a boat and drove it out to Pelican Bay where we now live.

I saw where Jim was playing at Bert's Bar in Matlacha. It billed itself as the ultimate dive bar with a million dollar view. That's my kind of place. Jim recognized us and we spoke. As we exchanged pleasantries he said, "Wait a minute, I'll be right back." He returned with another couple who also lived in Maryland. Introductions were made and we spent the rest of the show drinking and sharing stories. They became fast friends, thanks to Jim. Later, when we made our move to Punta Gorda, we stayed in their condo while boat shopping. They acted as our tour guides and mentors while we were still new in town. They remain great friends to this day.

I can't count how many other fine people we've met along the way thanks to Jim and his music. There are so many that we now call friends who we met at one of his shows. They further enrich our wonderful lives.

Seeking Something More

It wasn't always this way. I lived like everyone else. I had a good job, but I had grown to hate it. I had bills, lots of them. There was rent to pay, truck payment, credit card bills and the accumulation of stuff. It was cold in the winter and it snowed a lot. I had good friends, a few of them great. I had a good, normal life. I was trudging along like everyone does.

I did everything life asked of me. I worked hard, won some measure of success. I bought whatever toys I thought I wanted. It never seemed like it was enough. Is that all there is to life? I had a pretty wife who loved me. I had a great daughter I was proud of. She was all grown up and a great parent herself. The job was secure. I probably could have stayed on until proper retirement or death, except that it was driving me insane.

I couldn't shake the feeling that there ought to be something more. I found myself daydreaming more and more. I fantasized about chucking it all and running away. I explored job opportunities in Florida. I researched boats on the internet.

Not that I wasn't happy. I felt fortunate. I had it better than most and I knew it. There was just some inner yearning for freedom. As good as my life was, it wasn't exactly what I had planned. I just sort of ended up there. Through choices both good and bad, circumstances unforeseen, and good luck and bad luck, one day you wake up and realize this is where you ended up. That's how it works for most everyone.

It became clear to me that most folks, if they even realize the same thing, simply choose to accept their fate. Keep on keeping on. Keep showing up for work. Pay the bills. Save a little something for retirement if you live that long. Put one foot in front of the other. Get out of bed. Go to work. Watch television. Go to bed. Rinse and repeat.

It's just the way the world works. What else is there? I pondered that question for a long time. The daydreaming continued. The island songs played on. The job felt more and more like an anchor all the time. Did I mention it snowed a lot?

I wish I could tell you about one single moment when I had a great epiphany, that instant in time when I said,

"Screw it. I'm quitting my job and going off to live on a boat." It didn't work that way. Society itself was holding me back. The normal, responsible thing to do was keep trudging right along. Hold on to all you've worked for. Accept your fate. Settle in to your middle class American existence. Hope you don't get cancer before you can retire for a few years in your old age.

Yes I pondered all that endlessly, especially the cancer possibility. My mother lost a brief and brutal battle with breast cancer at the age of fifty-seven. My sister got to live to the ripe old age of fifty before kidney and liver cancer took her. Dad actually did get to retire. He got almost ten years of living his dream before pancreatic cancer took him at seventy-two. So I figured I had twenty more years optimistically. Possibly I had a whole lot less.

How was I going to live it? I needed to find a way to chart my own course. I couldn't let life decide for me how thing were going to turn out. I wanted to control my own destiny. I wasn't quite sure how, but I was going to figure it out. I was going to live life as I chose.

To find out how they made their dreams happen, and to read more of their tales of adventure, purchase Leap of Faith / Quit Your Job and Live on a Boat at Amazon.com, available in paperback or Kindle versions.

Ed Robinson

Weather Center
Web Cams
Yacht Clubs
About Us

CPSIA information can be obtained
at www.ICGtesting.com
Printed in the USA
LVOW01s1114131215
466478LV00023B/984/P